The Book of *Exodus*

LIVES OF GREAT RELIGIOUS BOOKS

The Book of *Exodus*, Joel S. Baden

The Book of *Revelation*, Timothy Beal

The *Dead Sea Scrolls*, John J. Collins

The *Bhagavad Gita*, Richard H. Davis

John Calvin's *Institutes of the Christian Religion*, Bruce Gordon

The *Book of Mormon*, Paul C. Gutjahr

The Book of *Genesis*, Ronald Hendel

The *Book of Common Prayer*, Alan Jacobs

The Book of *Job*, Mark Larrimore

The *Koran* in English, Bruce B. Lawrence

The *Lotus Sūtra*, Donald S. Lopez, Jr.

The Tibetan Book of the Dead, Donald S. Lopez, Jr.

C. S. Lewis's *Mere Christianity*, George M. Marsden

Dietrich Bonhoeffer's *Letters and Papers from Prison*, Martin E. Marty

Thomas Aquinas's *Summa theologiae*, Bernard McGinn

The *I Ching*, Richard J. Smith

The *Yoga Sutra of Patanjali*, David Gordon White

Augustine's *Confessions*, Garry Wills

The *Talmud*, Barry Scott Wimpfheimer

FORTHCOMING

The *Analects* of Confucius, Annping Chin and Jonathan D. Spence

The Life of Saint Teresa of Avila, Carlos Eire

Josephus's *The Jewish War*, Martin Goodman

Dante's *Divine Comedy*, Joseph Luzzi

The Greatest Translations of All Time, Jack Miles

The Letters of Paul, Margaret M. Mitchell

The Passover *Haggadah*, Vanessa Ochs

The *Song of Songs*, Ilana Pardes

The *Daode Jing*, James Robson

Rumi's *Masnavi*, Omid Safi

The Book of *Exodus*

A BIOGRAPHY

Joel S. Baden

PRINCETON UNIVERSITY PRESS

Princeton and Oxford

Published by Princeton University Press
41 William Street, Princeton, New Jersey 08540
6 Oxford Street, Woodstock, Oxfordshire OX20 1TR

press.princeton.edu

Library of Congress Control Number: 2018957588
ISBN 978-0-691-16954-5

British Library Cataloging-in-Publication Data is available

Editorial: Fred Appel, Thalia Leaf
Production Editorial: Terri O'Prey
Text Design: Lorraine Doneker
Jacket/Cover Design: Lorraine Doneker
Jacket Art: Jacob Lawrence, *The Migrants Arrived in Great Numbers*,
1940. © 2018 The Jacob and Gwendolyn Knight Lawrence Foundation,
Seattle /Artists Rights Society (ARS)
Production: Erin Suydam
Publicity: Tayler Lord, Kathyrn Stevens
Copyeditor: Cathryn Slovensky

This book has been composed in Garamond Premier Pro

Printed on acid-free paper. ∞

Printed in the United States of America

10 9 8 7 6 5 4 3 2 1

For my grandmother, Beatrice Gitlin,

who celebrates her ninety-eighth Passover this year

CONTENTS

ACKNOWLEDGMENTS

A book such as this, which ranges far from my native scholarly field, is necessarily made possible only with the support of friends and colleagues. I am grateful to all those who took the time to read portions of the manuscript, saving me from any number of errors and oversights. These include Harry Attridge, Andrew McGowan, Marc Brettler, Bruce Gordon, and Benjamin Valentin.

I am also deeply indebted to my graduate student assistants, without whom the project could not have been either started or completed: Laura Carlson, Harley Roberts, and James Nati.

Candida Moss is, as always, my constant intellectual companion, for which I am always thankful.

My daughters, Zara and Iris, are the ever-brilliant lights of my life, for whom I do all things.

This book is dedicated to my grandmother, who still sings the Four Questions in Yiddish at every Passover—proof of the enduring and ever-adaptive nature of the Exodus, and, at ninety-eight, of her own endurance as well.

The book of Exodus is the second book of the Hebrew Bible, but it may rank first in lasting cultural importance. It is in Exodus that the classic biblical themes of oppression and redemption, of human enslavement and divine salvation, are most dramatically and famously expressed. Many of the Bible's most famous characters and episodes are found here: Moses, Aaron, and Miriam, the burning bush, the ten plagues, the Passover, the crossing of the sea, the revelation and law-giving on Mount Sinai, the Ten Commandments, the golden calf. The story of suffering, escape, and journey through the wilderness toward the promised land was the defining narrative for ancient Israel and has maintained a central position in Western culture ever since. This book will trace that story through some of its most prominent and fascinating permutations, showing how Exodus has been adopted and adapted in numerous and often unexpected ways across space and time.

Before we begin, one important clarification is necessary. A distinction must be made between the biblical book of Exodus—the text that comes between Genesis and Leviticus and constitutes one-fifth of the canonical Pentateuch or Torah—and the Exodus story. The biblical book is but one, relatively late, stage in the development of the Exodus story. As the first chapter below will argue, what we call the book of Exodus is a somewhat artificial delineation of material within the Pentateuch, one that comprises much, but not all, of the material that we commonly associate with the overarching narrative of the Exodus. Moreover, the biblical book, while containing the central core of the Exodus story, is among the most variegated in the Bible. It also includes poems, law codes, architectural plans, and rituals. Each of these has had its own interpretive trajectory—especially the extensive description of the tabernacle, which occupies nearly a quarter of the biblical text of Exodus and provides the foundation for, among other things, the traditional Jewish definition of what constitutes forbidden work on the Sabbath. Similarly, many of the individual episodes and characters within the story could be the subjects of their own biographies. This book cannot contain such multitudes. And, as interesting as they are, these various elements are all overshadowed in the history of interpretation by the grand narrative in which they are set.

That grand narrative—the movement from Egypt to Canaan, from oppression to freedom—extends beyond the borders of the biblical book to which it lent its name. Its themes appear outside of the book of Exodus, indeed outside of the Pentateuch altogether, and often in forms that predate the composition of the pentateuchal text. Just as the traditional nativity story performed and displayed every Christmas season is not derived from a single New Testament gospel but is a distillation, combination, and expansion of an underlying narrative, so too references to the Exodus story do not tend to reflect the exact contours of the biblical book of Exodus. For millennia, the Exodus has been understood as an event, a tradition, a cultural memory, and a metaphor. The biblical book is itself but one literary version of the Exodus. Though it may be authoritative for some, it is neither the first nor the last word.

It is not the book of Exodus but the Exodus story that has captured the imagination of audiences and interpreters from the biblical period to the present. It is the Exodus story that this volume will be primarily concerned with—though never forgetting that it is the manifestation of the story in the biblical book that is most famous and most influential. In the following pages, we will consider the ways in which individuals and groups, in the thousands of years since the story coalesced into the form we now know, have appropriated this story to be their story, have cast themselves or others into the biblical roles, and have used the themes of this story for their various ends.

Another prefatory note about the structure of this book: In a traditional biography, we would progress in straightforward chronological order through the development of the main character from birth (or just before) to the present. Although there will be a general chronological movement to this biography, the life Exodus has led is not so easily told in a straight line. The Exodus story has been employed for a variety of purposes, across a wide range of conceptual categories: ritual, theological, ethnological, political, and more. While some are obviously earlier or later than others—the Passover Seder is separated by nearly two thousand years from liberation theology, for instance—for the most part these categories developed contemporaneously, if not simultaneously, and moved along parallel trajectories rather than standing as points on a single interpretive line. Exodus is like a person who made a mark in multiple walks of life—political, for example, plus literary, musical, religious, and scientific—and so a purely chronological approach to a biography would be fractured and difficult to follow.

Instead, this biography will treat the life of Exodus thematically (although within broad chronological parameters). After an initial chapter describing, as any good biography should, the origin story of the subject, we will turn to the variety of uses to which the Exodus story was already being put in the biblical period, in both the Hebrew Bible and the New Testament (chapter 2). From there we will turn to the Exodus as ritual: the Passover in Judaism and the Eucharist in Christianity (chapter 3); to the centrality of Exodus, and particularly the Sinai event, for Jewish and Christian concepts of the law and the relationship between the two faiths (chapter 4); to the ways that the story has been taken up by communities looking to create or consolidate their identities by identifying themselves with the Israel of Exodus (chapter 5); to the prominence of the Exodus account in the civil rights movements of America (chapter 6); and finally to the development of liberation theology, a movement with social and political aims that grounds itself in the traditional story of Exodus (chapter 7).

What this book ultimately aims to demonstrate is not only the centrality of the Exodus story in so much of Western culture but its remarkable flexibility and malleability. This story of oppression and liberation, of law and covenant, of disobedience both civil and religious, has left its mark in ways both well known and largely unrecognized. With more than two thousand years' worth of material to cover, not every aspect of Exodus's life can be discussed or even mentioned. Nevertheless, it should be apparent that few books, few stories, have had the kind of wide and lasting impact that we see in the book and story of Exodus.

The Book of *Exodus*

FIG. 1: Satellite photograph of the Sinai Peninsula.

Before the Bible

The biblical book of Exodus is an unusually complex literary work, even by the standards of the Bible. Not only does it comprise a remarkable variety of literary genres—prose, poetry, ritual, law, architectural blueprint, genealogy—but, as we will see, it reflects a range of individual preliterary traditions and multiple literary hands. In no sense is the book of Exodus a unified composition.

Although this is no longer a startling revelation, it bears repeating here: Moses, despite the traditional positions of Judaism and Christianity, did not write the book of Exodus, or the rest of the Pentateuch. Nowhere in Exodus, or anywhere else in the Pentateuch, is it claimed otherwise. Moses is, without exception, presented as a character in the story, not as its author. He is referred to always in the third person; although Moses, like everyone else, speaks in the first person, such speeches are always introduced by "Moses said," the words of the omniscient narrator and, by extension, the implied author. The view that Moses was the author of the Pentateuch, and therefore its second book, emerged only in the postbiblical period, perhaps most plainly in the pronouncement of the rabbis of the Talmud: "Moses wrote his book." Yet this traditional claim has been regularly challenged, both from within and without normative Judaism and Christianity. In the twelfth century, the Jewish exegete Abraham Ibn Ezra began to challenge the Mosaic attribution of certain verses ("Moses died," for instance). Five hundred years later, the political philosopher Thomas Hobbes declared unequivocally that Moses did not write the Pentateuch. The arguments leveled against Mosaic authorship have multiplied exponentially since then. (Some particularly cheeky critics—in perhaps my favorite bit of reasoning—note the logical difficulties of believing that Moses could have written this verse in Numbers: "Moses was a very humble man—more so than anyone else on the face of the earth.")

The task, once Mosaic authorship is off the table, is to understand how the Pentateuch, in our case specifically Exodus, might more credibly have been composed—and, pushing further back in time, what preliterary traditions were taken up in the creation of the Exodus story, and what, if any, authentic historical events may lie behind those traditions.

To get to the root of the story—or to find out if there are any roots at all—we must work from the ground up by turning to the world of archaeology. Archaeology cannot answer every question: we will, for instance, never find archaeological evidence of any conversations, be they between Pharaoh and his servants, between Aaron and the people, or, most of all, between God and Moses. The burning bush, the golden calf, and even the tabernacle are beyond recovery. Individual actors may have left their mark on history, but we hope in vain to find any remains that can be identified as those of Moses, Aaron, or Miriam. So our leading question must be: What kind of evidence for the Exodus story might we justifiably expect archaeology to produce?

We must think big. This is a story, at least according to the biblical account, of a massive population of Israelites and its interactions, both servile and military, with a major civilization of the ancient Near East, Egypt. Taking the biblical story literally, at least for the moment, we are reckoning with more than six hundred thousand Israelite men of military age—thus, counting women, children, and the elderly, approximately two million Israelites in total, along with their possessions, including livestock, household goods, and personal belongings—who departed en masse from Egypt and proceeded to spend forty years in the wilderness between Egypt and Canaan. We are talking also, from Egypt's perspective, of the gain and loss of an enormous workforce, and, most notably, the wholesale destruction of the Egyptian army, including the death of the pharaoh himself. Individuals may not be discernible in the archaeological record; masses of people, however, generally are.

There are two major categories of data to explore: material artifacts and textual records. Within the first, we might well expect to find some material remains either from Israel's four hundred years in Egypt or from their forty years in the wilderness. These were, after all, humans, living human lives: building dwellings, consuming food, discarding waste, participating in communal celebrations, dying and being buried. We need think only of the various discoveries of Paleolithic remains in Africa, or Neanderthals in Europe, to recognize that even much smaller groups of people cannot avoid leaving some trace of themselves behind, be it only a single cave painting, a solitary jawbone, or a stray flint.

And yet, when it comes to the Israelites of the Exodus, either in Egypt or in the wilderness, we have nothing. Not a single material trace of Israel's presence has been discovered. I remember mentioning this phenomenon at a family Seder one Passover, and my grandmother clinging to hope: "Perhaps they just haven't found it yet." It must be admitted that the lack of material remains is an argument from silence: absence of proof is not proof of absence. But neither the settled regions of Egypt nor the Sinai desert are so large that we should have simply failed to discover the places that the Israelites would have lived and traveled. Especially in this era of aerial photography and Google Earth, it is hard to imagine that the material remains of two million Israelites can have slipped under the radar.

On the textual front, unsurprisingly, the situation is similar. Egypt, like many advanced ancient cultures, kept quite good records: lists of their successive kings, annals of their political and military engagements, even registers of the annual level of the Nile. In all of ancient Egypt's archival records, in all of its official correspondence, there is no mention either of the wholesale enslavement of the Israelite people or of their precipitous departure. There is not a word about the land being ravaged by a succession of plagues or of the death of Pharaoh and his entire army at the sea. It might be argued that such embarrassments were swept under the carpet in Egypt's formal records, but it seems rather unlikely that the miraculous watery demise of a pharaoh could be easily glossed over.

If the archaeological evidence suggests that the Exodus story did not take place as described in the Bible, this does not necessarily mean that there is no factual basis at all for the narrative.[1] As has frequently been observed, it is difficult to imagine that the Israelites invented from whole cloth an origin story of enslavement and escape. In part, this is because the story is so unflattering: Who, given the chance to invent their past, would choose to have it begin in abject submission? We can, in fact, compare the Exodus with Israel's alternative origin story: that of the patriarchs, recounted in Genesis. Many scholars have concluded that these two stories were originally distinct: The tales of the patriarchs, in which Israel's ancestors are promised the land and move from place to place in Canaan setting down roots (building altars, purchasing land, burying their dead), represent one explanation for how Israel came to occupy its territory, and the story of the Exodus, in which the Israelites enter Canaan as a conquering army from outside the land, represents another.[2] The patriarchal story is conceivably the kind of past that a people would invent for themselves. If not triumphant, it is at least entirely positive. The Exodus story, with its depiction of the Israelites as foreign subjects, suffers by contrast.

Another point against the wholesale invention of the Exodus story is the identity of the oppressing nation. For most of its history—at least the periods in which the biblical texts were written—Israel was under the thumb of a series of foreign rulers: the Arameans, the Assyrians, the Babylonians, the Persians, the Greeks, and the Romans. The Exodus account is understandable as a commentary on the experience of foreign domination, but we might expect that its creators would choose a foreign power that had a semblance of cultural resonance in their day and age. The choice of Egypt is therefore curious: Egypt, for the most part, was also under the control of this succession of empires. (We might think of Isaiah's pejorative assessment of Egypt's power in the Assyrian period: "that broken reed of a staff.")

Yet in the very early period of Israel's history—before Israel could even really be called a coherent community—Egypt was in fact the dominant power in Canaan. In the late second millennium BCE, most of Canaan's major city-states—including Megiddo, Shechem, and Jerusalem—were vassals of Egypt's New Kingdom pharaohs. The first recorded mention of Israel's existence is in an Egyptian stele from the late thirteenth century BCE, in which the pharaoh Merneptah includes Israel in a list of conquered peoples. Although the biblical authors can hardly be expected to have known this distant history, the Exodus story may well preserve a long-standing cultural memory of Egyptian power and Canaanite subjugation—a distant recollection, filtered through centuries of oral tradition, and shaped to suit the needs and knowledge of each generation.

Egyptian records may not contain any references to the enslavement of an entire Israelite population, but we do have evidence that some Semitic people—individuals and small groups, perhaps—were indeed put to work in Egypt. There are pictorial depictions of Egyptian slaves, employed in building projects, with stereotypically Semitic clothing and hairstyles. A list of servants owned by a wealthy Egyptian woman reveals that more than half bore Semitic names.

More tantalizing still are the occasional letters that have been discovered, written by slave owners to the officers stationed at border fortresses on the way to Canaan, requesting assistance in tracking down and returning runaway slaves: "Send word to me about the whole story with them and how many people you had go after them."[3] These letters name no more than one or two individuals, but together with other fleeting images they do paint a very rough picture. There were Semitic slaves in Egypt, and occasionally they tried to escape to Canaan.

This may be a far cry from the epic narrative of Exodus, but it does provide us with a potential kernel for the biblical story—and, moreover, one that would square with the archaeological evidence (or lack thereof). A onetime mass exodus of all Israelites from Egypt cannot be maintained, but a relatively steady trickle of Semitic slaves making their way through the Sinai to the northeast seems eminently reasonable. Upon arriving in Canaan, these refugees would have found their natural place not in the cosmopolitan centers along the coast—the territory of the Philistines beginning in the twelfth century or so—but, more likely, in the less densely populated hill country, alongside a small but growing community that was gradually settling there and defining itself against its Canaanite origins: the nascent Israelites.[4]

For the experience of a handful of Egyptian runaways to become the epic narrative of the Bible, three processes likely took place: exaggeration, assimilation, and accretion. The first, exaggeration, is perhaps the easiest to understand. A simple escape becomes a story of divine salvation as easily as a thunderstorm becomes the path of the deity wreaking destruction, an overflowing of the Euphrates becomes the myth of a primordial global flood, a pile of ruins becomes the narrative of a triumphant conquest. At a time when no distinction was made between "natural" and "supernatural," and when everything from the weather to politics to one's individual life story was understood as controlled, or at least condoned, by heavenly forces, the small victory of successfully escaping from the clutches of a great empire would have been more than worthy of commemoration.

It is through assimilation that the personal stories of these former slaves were combined to become the corporate story of Israel. As the refugees from Egypt intermarried with the native Israelite population, they participated in the process known as fictive kinship: the blending of individual and family and community narratives into a single, increasingly complex past. Such blending happened on multiple levels throughout Israel's early history. The localized communities who traced their ancestry back to a patriarch named Abraham joined with those who remembered their forefather Isaac, and those who knew of an ancestor named Jacob, to create the fictive lineage we see in Genesis. And these native groups, with their accumulated multigeneration patriarchal traditions, assimilated into their narrative the story of an escape from Egypt—thereby creating the somewhat stilted, overarching story of patriarchal promise and settlement, forced abandonment of God-given territory, enslavement and escape, and glorious return to the promised land.

The third process is that of accretion. How was a barebones tale of escape and travel through the desert to Canaan expanded into the rich and diverse narrative we see in the biblical text? In the telling and retelling of their story, the early Israelites took up a wide range of traditional narratives and themes, fitting them in and reshaping the whole as they went. Ancient Near Eastern cultures often depicted their deities as warriors, as did Israel (one may think particularly of the ancient hymn in Habakkuk 3, with the verse reading "Pestilence marches before him, and plague comes forth at his heels" [verses 4–5]);[5] this warrior-god tradition stands behind the narrative of the plagues in Exodus. The mythic theme of the warrior-god's battle against the sea—common to both Mesopotamian and Canaanite traditions—informs the story of the Egyptians meeting their fates in the depths of the Sea of Reeds (see Isaiah 51:10, a reference to creation, but eminently relevant to the Exodus account: "It was you that dried up the Sea, the waters of the great deep / that made the abysses of the Sea a road the redeemed might walk"). The various miracles of sustenance in the wilderness—manna, water from a rock, bitter waters turned sweet—belong to a tradition that stretches from the early biblical prophets Elijah and Elisha into the New Testament and beyond.

The event that stands at the heart of the book of Exodus, the revelation at Sinai, is also most likely a tradition that originated independently of the Exodus proper.[6] Like the story of enslavement and escape, this episode is probably the product of an experience that took on layer upon layer of added meaning. Whether inspired by a thunderstorm atop a desert mountaintop or some similar phenomenon, we can imagine a group that bore the story of their theophanic experience with them to the community and narrative of early Israel. The probability that this community was not the same as the one that left Egypt is largely due to the location of the mountain of revelation in the tradition. The biblical Mount Sinai is traditionally identified as the mountain that bears the same name today, in the Sinai Peninsula (which is named after the mountain). But that identification stems only from the fourth century CE, when Helena, the mother of the emperor Constantine, declared it so, and ordered a chapel to be built on the site. (Helena was also responsible for "identifying" other major holy sites, including the Church of the Holy Sepulchre in Jerusalem.) Some of our oldest biblical texts, however, locate Sinai not to the southwest of Canaan but to the southeast: Deuteronomy 33 places it in Seir, another name for Edom. Traditions describe the southern mountain as Yahweh's original home. The Exodus and Sinai traditions, with their common wilderness setting, were readily integrated. Yet the seams still show: in the narrative of Israel's rescue from Egypt there is little hint that they will be brought anywhere other than Canaan—yet they find themselves heading first, unexpectedly, and in no obvious geographical order, to an obscure mountain.

To the mountain tradition was added the equally independent tradition of the law-giving, which could hardly have been an original part of the theophanic experience, whatever the latter's "natural" origins. Law codes were a long-standing Near Eastern genre. The dependence of the legal corpus in Exodus, in particular on those of the neighboring Hittite and especially Mesopotamian civilizations, is indisputable, the parallels at times verging on the verbatim. (Compare the early second-millennium Akkadian law code of Eshnunna, "If an ox gores another ox and thus causes its death, the two ox-owners shall divide the value of the living ox and the carcass of the dead ox," to the nearly identical law in Exodus 21:35: "When a man's ox injures his neighbor's ox and it dies, they shall sell the live ox and divide its price; they shall also divide the dead animal."[7]) The same is true of the sacrificial rites, found partly in Exodus and in fullest expression in Leviticus, which have strong parallels with cultic texts discovered at the Canaanite city of Ugarit.[8]

A word is necessary here about the figure of Moses, who dominates both the story and the biblical book of Exodus. There is good reason to think that Moses was an integral part of the earliest Exodus traditions, the core or kernel of the narrative. Most probative in this regard is the most basic fact about the man: his name. Moses is an Egyptian word meaning, simply, "son." It is well known even to people with only minimal knowledge of ancient Egypt. It is the same word we see in the names of some of history's most famous pharaohs, including Thutmose III ("son of Thoth," the Egyptian ibis-headed god), who reigned alongside and following Queen Hatshepsut; and Ramesses II ("son of Ra," the Egyptian sun god), known more widely as Ramesses the Great. Many aspects of the beginning of the book of Exodus—the identification of Moses's Levite parents, his extensive genealogy, and the story of his being raised (and named) by Pharaoh's daughter—seem to be attempts to overcome the possibility that the great leader of the Israelites may not, in fact, have been an Israelite at all. These efforts testify, at the very least, to the antiquity of Moses's place in the Exodus tradition. Were he a late invention, there would be no need to have given him an Egyptian name, much less to try and account for it in multiple ways.

As the Exodus story expanded to become the central narrative of Israel's history, the figure of Moses expanded along with it, incorporating elements from different traditions in an attempt to make the man worthy of his context. We have already mentioned the concept of the law-giving, which in biblical and postbiblical tradition became synonymous with Moses (such that the New Testament could make reference to the law books of the Pentateuch merely by saying "Moses," as in, for example, Luke 24:27). Moses was provided with a tale of marriage that is patterned on the traditional type-scene of the meeting at the well, known to us from the patriarchal stories of Isaac/Rebekah and Jacob/Rachel. He was configured as the prototypical prophet, complete with a call narrative formally similar to those of Samuel, Isaiah, and other traditional Israelite prophetic figures. Moses takes on both royal and priestly roles as well, serving as judicial authority and oracular voice, officiating in both civil and cultic spheres. By the time the text of Exodus reached its final form, the figure of Moses had been stuffed to the point of saturation.

All of this—the exaggeration, assimilation, and expansion of the kernel of an experience into the epic of the Exodus narrative—took place on the oral, preliterary level. We are dealing here not with a scribal process of writing and rewriting but with storytelling: the bringing together of individuals and communities, with their disparate experiences and stories, into a single community with a single story. The Exodus account, like the patriarchal tales, became part of Israel's collective cultural memory. As such it became, paradoxically, both fixed in the tradition and malleable in the hands of individual interpreters and communities of interpretation. For while a basic outline of the story may have been held in common—oppression in Egypt, the leadership of Moses, the departure and encounter with God at the mountain, the journey through the wilderness toward Canaan—the details of the plot, the themes to be emphasized, the ideologies to be promoted, were, as is always the case when it comes to stories, at the mercy of the teller.

In chapter 2, we will explore the variety of ways that the Exodus story found expression across the Hebrew Bible and the New Testament. Here, however, our interest lies in the diversity that is concentrated precisely where we might expect to find uniformity: in the canonical book of Exodus.

The "book of Exodus" is something of a misnomer. Historically, no such independent work ever existed—no one wrote something called "Exodus," or "Shemot" (the Hebrew name for the book). The text that we designate by these labels is, and always has been, nothing other than the second volume of a five-volume work: the Pentateuch, or Torah. The division of the Pentateuch into five volumes was a function of material concerns: ancient scrolls were incapable of holding such a vast work.[9] (This is akin to, say, modern printed encyclopedias. Although they may come in multiple volumes, no one would think that "C–D" is a literary work independent of the rest of the *Encyclopaedia Britannica*.) This does not mean that the beginning and end of Exodus are entirely arbitrary, of course. Knowing that a break has to be placed somewhere, it makes good sense to begin Exodus just after the death of Joseph and just before the beginning of the Israelite oppression in Egypt, just as it makes good sense to end it with the completion of the tabernacle. But the artificiality of the book division remains evident. Exodus begins with the phrase "And these are the names," with that revealing conjunction "and"; the book that follows Exodus, Leviticus, begins with the words "He called to Moses"—an "opening" that is sensible only if we know, from the end of Exodus, that God is the subject of the verb.

In terms of literary history, then, the Pentateuch is the main object of inquiry, and the book—the volume—of Exodus merely participates in the same literary developments that are evident across the whole. As scholars have recognized for more than two hundred years now, the Pentateuch as a whole is a composite work.[10] Its disunity is evident from the regular and thoroughgoing contradictions, duplications, and narrative inconsistencies discernible on the most basic level—that of the plot. The two creation stories of Genesis 1 and 2 provide the opening salvo. It is impossible to read them as a single unified narrative, as they disagree on almost every point, from the nature of the precreation world to the order of creation to the length of time creation took. Moreover, the distinctive claims of each creation story are followed through in subsequent chapters of Genesis, which are themselves contradictory. The most famous example of this phenomenon is the flood story in Genesis 6–9, which comprises two very different flood stories that have been woven together into a single, almost unintelligible narrative. Each of the two flood stories picks up on one of the two creation stories. These are not independent units but parts of originally continuous larger wholes.

Following both the contradictions and the continuities in the narrative of the Pentateuch from beginning to end reveals not two but four separate source documents from which the final text was composed. In order of appearance in the Bible, these are designated as P, for the Priestly source, which begins in Genesis 1 and contains, among much else, the vast cultic legislation of Leviticus; J, for Jahwist (the German spelling of Yahwist), the source that begins in Genesis 2 and includes the famous promise to Abraham in Genesis 12; E, for Elohist, which enters the picture in the story of Abraham and contains the story of the sacrifice of Isaac in Genesis 22; and, finally, D, for Deuteronomist, which is found exclusively in Deuteronomy and constitutes the vast majority of the Pentateuch's final book. All of these originally independent documents hold in common the general outlines of the pentateuchal narrative: the sequence of Abraham, Isaac, and Jacob, followed by the Joseph story, oppression in Egypt, the Exodus, the revelation at the mountain, wandering in the wilderness, and the eventual arrival at the eastern border of the promised land. But once we move beyond this traditional order of events, virtually every detail differs from source to source. Stories that we think of as fundamental to the Bible are often known to, or at least told by, only one biblical author—the sacrifice of Isaac, for example, is found in E but not even alluded to in passing by anyone else.

It is typical—indeed, almost universal—for biblical readers and interpreters to smooth out the problems in the narrative. This is in part a function of the assumptions we bring to reading. When we pick up a book, we expect it to be coherent, and even unconsciously we try to elide any discontinuities we encounter.[11] It is also a function of the Bible's place in our religious heritages. Whether due to traditions of Mosaic authorship or simply from the need to find a unified and unifying message in the Bible, faith-based exegesis of the text often strives quite openly to mitigate any potential inconsistencies. Yet when we read the Pentateuch—in this case the book of Exodus—without these assumptions and expectations, it swiftly becomes apparent that a unified reading of the text is difficult to maintain.

In the very first chapter, Pharaoh's schemes to oppress the Israelites seem to be at odds with themselves. If Pharaoh desires the Israelites as slave labor, what is the purpose of attempting to kill them off by murdering every male child? What is the name of Moses's father-in-law: Reuel, as in Exodus 2, or Jethro, as in Exodus 3? In Exodus 3 God reveals his proper name, Yahweh, to Moses; in Exodus 6 he does so again. In Exodus 4 Moses and Aaron speak to the Israelites, who are convinced that God has finally taken notice of their misery; in Exodus 6, Moses and Aaron present the same message again to the Israelites, but the Israelites do not listen. Twice, in Exodus 4 and 6, Moses complains of his inability to speak well; twice God declares that Aaron will be Moses's mouthpiece. In the plague of blood, Moses tells Pharaoh that he, Moses, will strike the Nile and turn it to blood; God then instructs Aaron to hold his staff over the waters of Egypt and turn them all to blood. Throughout the plagues, Moses makes the famous demand of Pharaoh— "Let my people go"—yet at the same time God is busy hardening Pharaoh's heart in order to prevent that very release. In some passages, the Israelites dwell in the set-apart region of Goshen, yet when it is time for the death of the firstborn, the Israelites must distinguish their houses from those of their Egyptian neighbors by putting blood on the lintels and doorposts. At the crossing of the sea in Exodus 14, God declares that Pharaoh will pursue the Israelites only after God has hardened his heart, yet Pharaoh then goes ahead and pursues the Israelites before God has hardened his heart—and then again after. When the Israelites see the Egyptians approaching, Moses tells them to stand still; God then tells them to move forward. At the theophany at the mountain, the people have to be both restrained from rushing toward God and led reluctantly toward the mountain. The sound of the horn is said to signal both the beginning of the theophany and the moment when it is safe to approach the mountain. After the law-giving, God tells Moses to come up the mountain, but Moses instead returns to the people and offers sacrifices. The instructions for the tabernacle describe a tent of meeting at the center of the Israelite camp, in which God will dwell, and that no human may enter, yet Exodus 33 describes the tent of meeting as being outside the Israelite camp, and Moses and Joshua regularly enter it.

There are seemingly simple questions that have no obvious answer: How many children does Moses have, and when does he have them? What is Moses's relationship with Aaron, or Miriam? What is Aaron's relationship with Miriam? What is the mountain of revelation called—Horeb or Sinai? What did Moses receive there—laws, blueprints, a covenant?

These are only some of the issues raised by the text, but they are enough to illustrate the breadth of problems encountered in any straightforward reading. The narrative in the book of Exodus presents contradictory viewpoints, indeed contradictory plot points, about matters both large and small. When understood as part of the composite Pentateuch, this is only to be expected. The book of Exodus is, more accurately, the combination of three different Exodus stories—three literary manifestations of the underlying Exodus tradition, each building on a common foundation but erecting very different conceptual and even narrative edifices. An examination of each of these Exodus stories will illustrate just how wide the gap is between them—and just how distinctive each is, not just from one another, but from what we think of as the "standard" story of the Exodus.

The P narrative opens by recalling the descent of Jacob and his family to Egypt and their proliferation there, all of which had already been described by P in Genesis. The enslavement of the Israelites by Pharaoh is a response to their fertility: they are made to do all sorts of labor, both in construction work and in the field. When the Israelites cry out, God hears them and remembers his covenant with the patriarchs Abraham, Isaac, and Jacob.

Moses is introduced into the story without any fanfare or explanation of why he is the one chosen, but only with a genealogy. Immediately, God addresses Moses with the revelation of God's proper name, Yahweh, and with the promise to deliver the Israelites from their bondage. When Moses pleads an inability to speak well, Aaron is designated as his prophet, and the two of them make their way to Pharaoh to perform a series of signs and wonders: the plagues. In P, there are seven wonders—Aaron's staff turning into a crocodile (not a serpent, as it is frequently mistranslated), the waters of Egypt turning to blood, frogs, lice, boils, hail, locusts, and darkness—followed by the death of the firstborn, complete with the proto-Passover daubing of blood on the doorposts and lintels so that God will know to protect (the authentic meaning of the word *pesah*, traditionally translated as "pass over") the houses of the Israelites.

The plagues in P are not intended to convince Pharaoh to let the people go; indeed, by hardening Pharaoh's heart, God ensures that even if the Egyptian king wanted to let the Israelites go he would be unable to do so. Pharaoh has no free will in the P plagues. The signs and wonders (P never uses the word "plague" or its equivalent) exist to demonstrate God's power—so that "the Egyptians shall know that I am Yahweh." There is no time between the plagues for Pharaoh to change his mind, even if he could; each follows upon the other in direct succession, without any intervening dialogue between Moses and Pharaoh. The wonders are a series of punches to the gut of Pharaoh and Egypt, and when the last one has struck, the death of the firstborn, the Israelites simply depart in broad daylight, "with a high hand," that is, brazenly—there is no sense of hurry, no unleavened bread. Pharaoh does not let them go; they just go.

The famous episode of the splitting of the sea in P is depicted much as it is in popular culture, in movies such as *The Ten Commandments*: Moses raises his staff, the Israelites walk through on dry ground, and, when the Egyptians enter, the waters return and drown them. But the P narrative makes clear that this, too, happened essentially against Pharaoh's will. God hardened Pharaoh's heart to force his decision to pursue the Israelites into the wilderness, and hardened the hearts of the Egyptians as a whole to force them to pursue the Israelites into the midst of the water. There is no suspense in the P story, here or anywhere. The events are an illustration of God's power, and everything happens exactly according to plan.

The account of the revelation at Sinai is told very briefly. The glory of God appears in a cloud on top of the mountain, and Moses ascends to enter the cloud. There he receives neither laws nor a covenant; what God gives Moses on top of Sinai is the blueprint for God's future dwelling place: "Let them make me a sanctuary that I may dwell among them" (Exod 25:8). For seven full chapters we are presented, in excruciating detail, with the specifics of the tabernacle. Once Moses has the blueprint, he returns to the people, his face radiant from his encounter with the deity (this is the origin of the tradition that Moses had horns, as the Hebrew words for "rays of light" and "horns" are the same). We then have another six full chapters describing, in excruciating detail, how the people carried out the divine building plans, culminating with the climactic statement of the P source in Exodus, and perhaps in the entire Pentateuch: "When Moses had finished the work, the cloud covered the Tent of Meeting, and the glory of Yahweh filled the Tabernacle" (Exod 40:33–34; NJPS uses "Presence" rather than "glory").

In J's Exodus narrative, we begin with the deaths of Joseph and his brothers, and the rise of a pharaoh who did not remember Joseph's contributions to Egypt's survival. This new pharaoh is discomfited by the presence of an Israelite population in Egypt and determines to enslave them in order to prevent them from becoming too large. The plan backfires, however: "the more they were oppressed, the more they increased" (Exod 1:12). It is in this period of Israelite enslavement that Moses is born and grows up. When he is old enough to join his kinsmen in their labors, he sees an Egyptian beating a fellow Israelite, and kills the taskmaster. As news of the murder spreads, Moses flees to Midian, in the wilderness to the east of Egypt, and there he marries Zipporah.

When the oppressive pharaoh dies, God instructs Moses to return to Egypt. On the way, he encounters the deity in the burning bush and is given his marching orders: to gather the Israelite elders and demand that Pharaoh let the people go a three-days' journey into the wilderness to offer sacrifices to God. Moses tries his best to avoid his responsibility but is left with no choice after God grows angry and promises to send Aaron as Moses's spokesman. Moses and Aaron approach the new pharaoh and make their demand but are rebuffed. In fact, Pharaoh imposes even harsher labor on the Israelites. It is in response to Pharaoh's intransigence that God begins the cycle of the plagues.

J's narrative contains six plagues—the Nile turning to blood, frogs, swarms of insects, pestilence, hail, and locusts—followed by the death of the firstborn. The plagues in J, in contrast to the signs and wonders of P, are genuine attempts to convince Pharaoh to release the Israelites. Before each plague Moses announces the impending disaster; after each, Pharaoh agrees to let the Israelites go once the plague ends. But in every case Pharaoh changes his mind once he sees that there is relief. The Pharaoh of J has absolute free will; his stubbornness is entirely his own. It is also worth noting that the famous phrase "Let my people go" is never actually stated as a demand for complete freedom. It is always no more than a request to make a brief journey into the wilderness to sacrifice. It is, in short, a ruse, and one that Pharaoh falls for; even after the death of the firstborn, Pharaoh still expects the Israelites to return to Egypt. This is why, in J, the Israelites depart in haste, in the middle of the night, without even giving their dough time to rise. They know that Pharaoh might well change his mind again, and that they have to get away as far as possible and as fast as possible.

And indeed, when Pharaoh realizes that the Israelites will not be returning, he immediately gathers his chariots and pursues them. The story of the death of the Egyptians at the sea in J is very different from the one we are used to. In J, the Israelites are fleeing northeast along the coast of the Mediterranean—the shortest route from Egypt to Canaan. Instead of crossing through a body of water, they are instructed to stand still while God does their fighting for them. In the middle of the night, as the Egyptians are approaching, God sends an east wind to blow the great sea back, creating a false coastline. When in the morning the Egyptians take up their pursuit again, they continue to march along what they believe to be the path the Israelites took, but what is in reality the newly exposed seabed. God causes their chariots to stick in the mud, and, when they are right where he wants them, the sea returns to its natural place, swamping the Egyptian army with the equivalent of a massive tidal wave.

Once free of the Egyptian threat, the Israelites find themselves in a harsh wilderness, where they complain repeatedly about a lack of provisions. God gives them what they need—water and food (manna)—but also grows impatient as the people seem incapable of true faith: "Is Yahweh present among us or not?," they openly wonder (Exod 17:7). The theophany at Sinai in J is a response to this lack of faith: "Yahweh will come down in the sight of all the people, on Mount Sinai" (19:11). After confirming that the people may not approach the mountain while God is present there, God calls to Moses and invites him to ascend the mountain. There Moses again receives neither law nor covenant, nor even architectural plans. Moses is brought to the mountaintop only for God to tell him that it is time to leave Sinai— and, crucially, that God will not be personally accompanying the Israelites any farther, for they have proven themselves to be stiff-necked. Moses pleads with God, God relents, and, in a sign of favor, allows Moses to see more of God's physical presence—his back—than anyone else; but, God says, "you cannot see my face, for man may not see me and live" (33:20). The theophany in J is just that: almost pure theophany, without any accompanying revelations. And this moment, the ultimate proof that God is, indeed, in the midst of the people, is the conclusion of J's contribution to the book of Exodus.

Finally, there is the E narrative. In E, the Egyptian king does not attempt to enslave the Israelites; rather, he attempts to eliminate them entirely, to commit genocide through the killing of every male Israelite newborn. Moses, however, is spared by his mother, in the famous story of placing him in a basket in the Nile, where he is discovered by Pharaoh's daughter and raised in the palace. Sometime later, when Moses is grown, God calls to him from a mountain in the wilderness called Horeb. God commissions Moses to free the Israelites from Egypt, and, in order to bolster Moses's credentials with the people, reveals his proper name, Yahweh. Moses returns to Egypt, and—there appears to be a gap in the story. The next thing we know, the Israelites are leaving Egypt. It is possible that E once contained a significant narrative between Moses's return and the departure of the Israelites, one that has been lost to us in the long process of textual transmission (none of the pentateuchal sources has been preserved completely). At the same time, however, there are no later passages in E that seem to refer back to anything that might have happened in this ostensible gap. E, it seems, had no plagues story, no confrontation with Pharaoh, and, as it turns out, no destruction of the Egyptians at the sea. We can only assume that Moses carried out his mission: he led the Israelites out of Egypt—and they left, we are told, armed for war.

This is no stray detail, for the first thing the Israelites encounter upon leaving Egypt is a battle against the Bible's stereotypical wilderness enemy, the Amalekites. Once the battle is won, with the help of a divine miracle, Moses's father-in-law, Jethro, arrives on the scene. Seeing how burdened Moses is by having to adjudicate all the petty squabbles of the Israelites, Jethro suggests instituting a professional judiciary, chosen from Israel's trusted elders. And with that problem out of the way, the Israelites find themselves back at the mountain where God had first spoken to Moses: Horeb. In E, the theophany has a clear purpose: "I will come to you in a thick cloud," God says to Moses, "in order that the people may hear when I speak with you and so trust you ever after" (Exod 19:9). The divine revelation is meant as a moment of prophetic authorization for Moses, for the people to declare Moses their intermediary with God. And this is precisely what happens. When the theophany begins, the people are terrified, and Moses brings them reluctantly to the foot of the mountain. There they witness God speaking to Moses—pronouncing the Ten Commandments—and, wishing never to hear God's voice directly again, they give Moses the authority he requires to lead them: "You speak to us . . . and we will obey; but let not God speak to us, lest we die" (20:19 [Hebrew]; 20:16 [English]).

With his prophetic commission established, Moses then returns to the divine cloud and receives the set of laws known as the Covenant Code, spanning Exodus 21–23. The giving of these laws is the centerpiece of the E narrative. The Israelites come to the mountain, and Moses is given prophetic authority, for the purpose of laying these laws before the people and, importantly, having the people accept them as the divine will. And indeed, when Moses transmits the laws to the Israelites, they assent to them in their entirety: "All the things that Yahweh has commanded we will do!" (24:3). The laws are sealed in covenantal fashion, with a cultic ceremony, and Moses is called back up the mountain to receive the tablets of the law, the physical symbol of the covenant.

In Moses's extended forty-day absence, however, the people become nervous and construct the golden calf. The calf is not, as is often thought, an image of some other deity; it is, rather, an image of Israel's god, Yahweh: it is meant to replace Moses as a figur(in)e that the Israelites can view as a manifestation of the deity in their midst. In making the calf, they are violating not the first law of the Ten Commandments—"you shall have no other gods before me"—but rather the first law of the Covenant Code: "with me you shall make no gods of silver, nor shall you make for yourselves any gods of gold" (Exod 20:23 [Hebrew]; 20:20 [English]). It is because they have broken the covenant—its very first law even—that God grows so angry, and that Moses feels compelled to destroy the symbol of that covenant, the tablets that he bore down from the mountaintop. It is only after much pleading by Moses on behalf of the people, and appropriate punishments for the Israelites, that God relents and agrees to fulfill his promise to lead the people to Canaan.

After a brief digression to describe the tent of meeting—which in E's view is a site of oracular revelation, a plain tent that sits outside the camp and to which Moses goes whenever he requires divine guidance—Moses returns to the mountaintop to receive the second set of tablets. These are just like the first—containing the Ten Commandments and inscribed with the finger of God. With the new set of tablets in hand, and with the covenant between God and the people thus reaffirmed, the Israelites are ready to leave Horeb for Canaan.

All of the classic elements of the traditional Exodus story are contained in these three accounts—but none of them contains all of those elements, and, when read separately, each is in fact markedly different from the standard narrative. In P, the proliferation of the Israelites precedes their enslavement; in J, it follows; and in E, there is no enslavement at all, only attempted genocide. In E, Moses is raised in Pharaoh's palace; not so in either J or P. In E and P, the call of Moses includes the revelation of the divine name; in J, the divine name has been known since the very beginning of Genesis. In J, Moses has one son; in E, two; in P, Moses has no wife or offspring at all. J and P both have plagues, while E does not, but even the two plague stories are quite distinct, with different plagues and different intentions in each, and with neither, it should be noted, containing ten plagues—that number is reached only in the canonical account that combines the J and P versions. J and P both have the Egyptians perishing in water, but not in the same body of water or in the same way. The three theophanies could hardly be more different from one another in terms of the rationale for the appearance of the deity and in terms of what is transmitted to Moses on the mountaintop: a blueprint in P, a law code in E, and a sharp rebuke in J. The mountain does not even have a consistent name: Sinai in J and P but Horeb in E.

There is no burning bush in E or P. There is no Miriam in J or P. In P and J, Aaron is Moses's brother; in E, it is Aaron and Miriam who are siblings, and seemingly unrelated to Moses. Joshua appears in Exodus only in E. The tent of meeting, the dwelling place of God, stands in the center of the Israelite camp in P, but outside the camp, and with a very different function, in E; J, for its part, knows of no such tent. The Ten Commandments are only in E. The golden calf is only in E. The list of differences could go on, but the overall point should be clear enough: while the basic plot of oppression, departure, wilderness, and revelation is common to all three sources, there are innumerable points of disagreement about both the building blocks and the additional episodes that have been attached to the central story.

None of these independent Exodus stories is the Exodus story we know—but the Exodus story we know could not exist without all three of these independent accounts of it. Each has something important to contribute to the whole, even as each is a perfectly sensible whole in itself.

The literary analysis of Exodus, as it turns out, leads to the same conclusion that we reach through an examination of the archaeological record: the biblical story of the Exodus is not to be understood as historically accurate in any straightforward way. If the biblical authors did not agree on how the story went, then we cannot even fall back on the traditional view that the Bible is an unqualified source of truth. There are multiple versions of the truth presented here, even in the Bible itself. We are dealing not with history but with a story—and stories, even more than historical events, are susceptible to framing and shaping, reinterpretation and reapplication across space and time.

What the literary history of the book of Exodus illustrates is just how flexible the Exodus story was in ancient Israel. The book of Exodus, as part of the Pentateuch, was not compiled from its constituent sources until the fifth century BCE. For most of Israel's history, then, the Exodus story existed—or, better, coexisted—in multiple forms. The authors of P, J, and E put the Exodus story to work in expressing their individual perspectives: to establish the basis of the priestly cultic system, to condemn Israelite intransigence, to promote a legal vision, and more. The canonical text of

Exodus, in other words, already encodes within it the inherent malleability of the underlying story. In chapter 2, we will take up some of the larger themes of the Exodus story, both in the book of Exodus and elsewhere in the Bible, and we will see how biblical writers were already adopting this remarkable story for a variety of purposes.

FIG. 2: Dead Sea Scrolls fragment (4Q22 frg. 1) containing parts of Exodus 6:25–7:19. Courtesy of the Leon Levy Dead Sea Scrolls Digital Library; Israel Antiquities Authority. Photo by Shai Halevi.

The Exodus Story Outside
the Book of Exodus

The recognition of the Exodus story's power is by no means a recent phenomenon. Even outside of the canonical book of Exodus, the story of God's rescue of the Israelites from Egypt suffuses the Bible. The epic retellings of the narrative, as discussed in chapter 1, are confined to the Torah, to the book of Exodus proper. But other biblical authors— historians, prophets, psalmists—regularly referred back to the narrative, or to some of its constituent elements and themes. They did so not simply to retell the story but to reinforce their own ideologies and arguments. These early appropriations of the Exodus story are the forerunners of the later uses we will explore in the chapters that follow. The postbiblical use of the Exodus story for a wide range of theological, sociological, and political purposes is not an abuse of the Bible—it is, rather, an emulation of the Bible itself.

The Hebrew Bible

The annual celebration of the Exodus from Egypt—the festival of Passover—can be understood as a ritualizing of history: the turning of a historical event into a communal set of practices, with a series of established steps that invest the rite with a coherent meaning. Indeed, this ritualizing of the Exodus story is precisely what we will take up in chapter 3. It is somewhat counterintuitive, then, to realize that within the Bible itself, the situation is reversed: the festival of Passover is in fact a historicizing of ritual.

In some of the earliest texts of the Bible, such as Exodus 23:14–17, the Israelites are instructed to observe three pilgrimage festivals each year: the festival of unleavened bread, or matza; the festival of the harvest; and the festival of ingathering. These were, as their names make clear, agricultural celebrations. Ancient Israel was a predominantly agrarian society, and their central festivals were linked to the various stages of the agricultural cycle. (One of the earliest extrabiblical inscriptions we have from Israel is called the Gezer Calendar, and is nothing other than a list of the seasons and the agricultural processes that take place therein.) At these festivals, we may presume, the Israelites were to go to their local sanctuaries and offer thanks to their god for yet another successful season of planting and sowing.

Our interest is in the first of these: the festival of unleavened bread. Originally a celebration of the early spring barley harvest, a series of biblical authors linked this agricultural festival to a specific historical event: the Exodus from Egypt. This connection may have been triggered by the narrative idea that the Israelites were in such a rush to depart Egypt that they did not have time to let their dough become leavened—but we might note that nowhere in the narrative of Exodus itself is the haste of the Israelites presented as a justification for the weeklong consumption of matza. (Indeed, the specifically seven-day period of eating unleavened bread, mandated by Jewish tradition for the holiday of Passover, has no basis in the story at all.)

Even as the agricultural festival of unleavened bread became historicized through the link with the memory of the Exodus, it remained separate from the pesah, or Passover, ceremony. Though we now conflate these into a single celebration, the Bible is quite clear that they were conceptually distinct: the pesah was a one-night event, timed to the night when God slew the firstborn in Egypt, while the festival of unleavened bread is the seven days that follow. The artificial conjoining of these two distinct rituals can be seen even in a surface reading of Exodus 12: the first fourteen verses are entirely about the pesah rite, with no mention of the festival of unleavened bread; verses 15–20 are, vice versa, entirely about the unleavened bread, with no reference to pesah; verses 21–27 again focus exclusively on the pesah. The pesah, like the unleavened bread, also was not originally linked to the Exodus: given its etymology, from the word "protection," it was likely an annual communal sacrificial offering in appreciation of God's continuing care for his people.

The festival calendars found in the Pentateuch, in Leviticus, Numbers, and Deuteronomy, maintain this basic distinction, even though they all share the understanding that the two rites have become a single event. The pesah is a sacrifice, to be offered at the sanctuary, which is followed by the abstinence from consuming leaven for a week. Outside of the calendars, virtually every reference to the Passover ritual elsewhere in the Bible ignores the festival of unleavened bread entirely and focuses exclusively on the pesah sacrifice. Thus, in Numbers 9, we find the regulations for what an individual is to do if he or she is not in the proper state of purity to offer sacrifices when the established date for pesah comes around—the solution is to create a second pesah exactly one month later. In Joshua 5, when the Israelites have finally crossed the Jordan and entered the promised land, they offer the pesah sacrifice. In 2 Kings 23, we learn that King Josiah—described as the greatest king of Israel since David, and as a great religious reformer—offered the pesah sacrifice for the first time since the death of Joshua. Generations later, when the Israelites returned from the exile in Babylon, they too offered the pesah sacrifice (and observed the festival of unleavened bread), according to the book of Ezra.

Perhaps the reason that the pesah garnered more attention than the seven days of unleavened bread that followed it has to do with the practical difference between the two rituals: while abstaining from leaven is an individual practice, the pesah sacrifice was both public and communal. In this light, we can see not only how the pesah, and the entire Passover ritual complex, came to commemorate a historical event through ritual observance but also how that ritual observance came to play a part in the formation and self-definition of the Israelite community.

Every ritual, of course, has to do with identity: rituals work only within systems and societies that accept their meaning and efficacy. So too cultural and historical memory always entails the reinforcing of community. What is notable about the Passover ritual, and the cultural memory it invokes, is not that it is part of a broader system, which it undoubtedly is, but rather that of all the rituals and memories that were available in ancient Israel, and to the biblical authors, it was this one that came to be the strongest signifier, especially at moments of inauguration or renewal. When Joshua brings the Israelite people into the promised land, they do two things: they circumcise all the males (a rite that evidently fell out of practice during the forty years in the wilderness), and they offer the pesah sacrifice. When King Josiah attempts to instill in his people a new sense of obligation to follow God's laws, he offers the pesah sacrifice. When the Israelites return from the exile to start their communal life in the promised land once again, they offer the pesah sacrifice. Each of these moments is one not just of transition but of communal and indeed national renewal. The biblical authors are picking up on the idea that the Exodus from Egypt—the literal departure on that one miraculous night—was itself a new beginning, an important new stage in the history of the Israelite people: indeed, the very moment at which the Israelite people truly came into being.

The biblical prophets are particularly emphatic on this last point. The eighth-century prophet Hosea, setting aside the traditions of the patriarchs Abraham, Isaac, and Jacob, dates the relationship between Israel and Yahweh to the Exodus: "I, Yahweh, have been your God ever since the land of Egypt" (Hos 12:10). "Only I, Yahweh, have been your God ever since the land of Egypt.... I looked after you in the desert" (Hos 13:4, 5). Perhaps most strikingly, "I fell in love with Israel when he was still a child; and I have called him my son ever since Egypt" (Hos 11:1). Israel, as a nation, was born in Egypt, and spent its youth in the wilderness, as Jeremiah also affirms: "I accounted to your favor the devotion of your youth . . . how you followed me in the wilderness" (Jer 2:2). Just as every ancient people was identified by affiliation with its national deity, so too Israel. And Israel's relationship with

Yahweh, its national deity, was forged in the Exodus. Ezekiel recounts God's words, "When I made myself known to them in the land of Egypt, I gave my oath to them. When I said 'I am Yahweh your God,' that same day I swore to them to take them out of the land of Egypt into a land flowing with milk and honey" (Ezek 20:5–6).

Israel's national identity is configured in the Bible as the people who were taken from Egypt, and thus the very idea of Egypt takes on a distinctive connotation of otherness. In the chapters of Leviticus that deal with sexual impropriety, the prohibited practices are described as those of Egypt: "You shall not copy the practices of the land of Egypt where you dwelt" (Lev 18:3). Historically, we know that in fact Egyptians were no more likely than anyone else, including the Israelites themselves, to commit incest or any other sexually deviant behavior. By defining these forbidden practices as Egyptian, however, the biblical authors reinforce the caesura between Egypt and Israel: we are not them.

This is why one of the gravest errors made by the Israelites in the wilderness was to long for a return to Egypt: "You have rejected Yahweh who is among you, by whining before him and saying, 'Oh, why did we ever leave Egypt!'" (Num 11:20). Returning to Egypt, immediately after the Exodus or at any time thereafter (as the prophet Jeremiah argued vehemently), is an undoing of the act through which Israel achieved its very existence as a people. Israel is special precisely, perhaps solely, because it left Egypt, as King David recognized: "Who is like your people Israel, a unique nation on earth, whom God went and redeemed as his people?" (2 Sam 7:23).

This uniqueness, embodied by the redemption from Egypt, forms the basis for appeals to divine mercy. "Let not your anger, O Yahweh, blaze forth against your people, whom you delivered from the land of Egypt with great power and with a mighty hand," pleads Moses in the wake of the golden calf (Exod 32:11). When Solomon dedicates the temple in Jerusalem, he asks that, if the people should sin, Yahweh might forgive them, calling on God's memory of the Exodus: "Grant them mercy . . . for they are your very own people that you freed from Egypt, from the midst of the iron furnace" (1 Kgs 8:50–51). Across the Hebrew Bible, Israel's understanding of itself as the people of the Exodus, as the object of God's mighty act, is essential to how they conceive of their relationship with God.

Although we tend to connect the idea that the Jews are God's "chosen people" to the figure of Abraham, the biblical authors are almost unanimous in claiming that in fact Israel's status as "chosen" is to be connected to the Exodus. God says to Moses before the plagues, "I will take you to be my people, and I will be your God; and you shall know that I, Yahweh, am your God who freed you from the labors of the Egyptians" (Exod 6:7). The same idea recurs when the Israelites arrive at Sinai: "If you will obey me faithfully and keep my covenant, you shall be my treasured possession among all the peoples. Indeed, all the earth is mine, but you will be to me a kingdom of priests and a holy nation" (Exod 19:5–6).

If the Israelites are defined by the experience of the Exodus, so too Yahweh is defined by having brought it about. "I am Yahweh your God who brought you out of the land of Egypt," says God in the first declaration of the Ten Commandments. When, after the death of Solomon, King Jeroboam sets up sanctuaries to Yahweh in the cities of Dan and

Bethel, hoping to lure northern worshippers away from the southern site of Jerusalem, he inaugurates them with the same words: "This is your god, O Israel, who brought you up from the land of Egypt" (1 Kgs 12:28).

This identification of both Israel and Yahweh with the event of the Exodus is not merely celebratory; it is, rather, grounds for Israel's obligation to Yahweh. It is because Yahweh is the god of the Exodus, and Israel the people of the Exodus, that Israel is to be obedient to God. This notion finds its strongest expression in Leviticus 25: "It is to me that the Israelites are servants: they are my servants, whom I freed from the land of Egypt" (Lev 25:55). The word for "servants" here is the same in Hebrew as that for "slaves." In other words, Israel has been freed from servitude to the Egyptians only to enter into servitude to Yahweh. Although the Exodus story is nearly always held up as the paradigmatic narrative of freedom, for many biblical authors such an interpretation would be missing the point. The Exodus represented freedom from human bondage but brought with it the obligation to serve a new master in heaven.

The book of Deuteronomy emphasizes this point repeatedly. "You saw with your own eyes all the marvelous deeds that Yahweh performed. Keep, therefore, all the instruction that I command you today" (Deut 11:7–8). "Bear in mind that you were slaves in the land of Egypt and Yahweh your God redeemed you; therefore I enjoin this commandment upon you today" (Deut 15:15). "Beware lest your heart grow haughty and you forget Yahweh your God who freed you from the land of Egypt, the house of bondage" (Deut 8:14). When, on the eve of his death, Joshua exhorts the Israelites to continue to be obedient to Yahweh, they reply, "Far be it from us to forsake Yahweh and serve other gods! For it was Yahweh our God who brought us and our fathers up from the land of Egypt, the house of bondage" (Jos 24:16–17). When they do, in fact, forsake the Lord and serve other gods, at the beginning of the book of Judges, a divine messenger appears and proclaims in Yahweh's name, "I brought you up from Egypt and I took you into the land which I had promised on oath to your fathers. . . . But you have not obeyed me—look what you have done!" (Judg 2:1–2). When the northern kingdom of Israel is conquered and its inhabitants exiled, the author of the book of Kings could not be clearer about what went wrong: "This happened because the Israelites sinned against Yahweh their God, who had freed them from the land of Egypt, from the hand of Pharaoh, king of Egypt" (2 Kgs 17:7). Jeremiah declares, "When I freed your fathers from the land of Egypt . . . this is what I commanded them: Do my bidding, that I may be your God and you may be my people" (Jer 7:22–23). "Cursed be the man who will not obey the terms of this covenant, which I enjoined upon your fathers when I freed them from the land of Egypt" (Jer 11:3–4). Even in the book of Psalms the link between obedience and the Exodus is made: "It is a law for Israel, a ruling of the God of Jacob; he imposed it as a decree upon Joseph when he went forth from the land of Egypt" (Ps 81:5–6).

The rehearsals of and references to the Exodus in the Hebrew Bible—and there are many more that have not been directly mentioned here—all hearken back to the same fundamental narrative, but they do so in order to emphasize a range of broader issues. The importance of ritual, and the linking of ritual with history; the definition of Israel as a people and the formation of community; appeals to divine mercy; advocacy for adherence to the law—all are given expression through the Exodus story.

Second Temple Literature

The period roughly between the Greek conquest of Israel by Alexander the Great in 332 BCE and the destruction of the Second Temple in Jerusalem by Rome in 70 CE was a fertile one for Jewish literature, though much of it did not make it into our traditional biblical canons. As the texts from this era fall between the composition of the majority of the Hebrew Bible and the writing of the New Testament, however, they still belong to the "biblical" period writ large, and are worthy of attention. As was the case with the Hebrew Bible, for the Jewish authors in this Second Temple period the Exodus story was fertile ground for interpretation and reuse.

A common thread that runs through most of the Jewish literature of the Second Temple period is the need to confront new historical circumstances, in particular, the existential crisis caused by the dominance of Greek, and later Roman, culture. In the writings of the Second Temple period, we have authors who were living in the diaspora—in Alexandria, for example—as well as many authors who, though still living and writing in Israel, were all too conscious of the fact that their culture had been overwhelmed by the hellenizing trends that followed the conquests of Alexander the Great. In this context, questions of communal identity came to the forefront.

For some Jewish authors living in Alexandria, the biblical story of the Israelites in Egypt presented a parallel too close to ignore. This sense may have been exacerbated by the occasional flare-up of persecution against the Jews—one such moment being an anti-Jewish riot in 38 CE, instigated by members of the Alexandrian elite, who denigrated the local Jews as foreigners. Whether in direct response to such outbreaks of persecution or simply because they lived in Greco-Roman Egypt, we find writers who retold and interpreted the Exodus story as a means of linking the past and present, in order to understand themselves and their place in the very same foreign land.

One such writer was the anonymous author of the Wisdom of Solomon, a text probably from the first century BCE that is part of the canon of the Catholic and Eastern Orthodox Churches and is considered one of the apocryphal books for Protestants.[1] In this work the author draws a series of seven comparisons between the Israelites and the Egyptians, illustrating how God preserved his people in the wilderness by the same means through which he punished his enemies with the plagues. "They"—the Egyptians— "were killed by the bites of locusts and flies . . . but your children were not conquered even by the fangs of venomous serpents" (Wis 16:9–10). While these comparisons are couched as demonstrations of how God's wisdom works in the world, they also recognizably set up binary values: the righteous, Israel, and the wicked, Egypt. "The deliverance of the righteous and the destruction of their enemies were expected by your people" (18:7)—it is easy to see how this would have been meant not only as an explanation of the past but as a salve for the present. The Wisdom of Solomon describes the

Israelites in Egypt—in the past and, implicitly, in the author's present—as undeserving of their fate, and as oppressed by a thoroughly evil regime. This view is couched in the type of traditional wisdom-oriented worldview we see in Proverbs, in which everyone eventually gets what they deserve. In this way, the author of the Wisdom of Solomon uses the Exodus story to provide the audience with a sense of security that, no matter how bad it may seem, God will reward the righteous and punish the wicked.

While the Wisdom of Solomon was written for a Jewish audience, other authors were writing for their non-Jewish contemporaries, and taking quite a different approach in their use of the Exodus story. Greek writers of this period tended to denigrate Judaism as a religion and to reconceive some of the standard narratives of Jewish tradition, including the Exodus story. Moses, whose story was well known among pagan writers, was frequently portrayed as a charlatan who fooled his followers into believing that he had been sent by God. The Israelites were regularly described as a colony of lepers who were forcibly expelled from Egypt. These pagan authors seem to have recognized the importance of the Exodus story among their Jewish neighbors, and consciously turned it against them. In response to such allegations, Jewish authors attempted not only to counter these falsehoods but to present Moses, in particular, as a paragon of typical Hellenistic virtues.

The Jewish historian Josephus—perhaps best known for his account of the siege and mass suicide at Masada—wrote in Rome in the first century CE. He emphasizes Moses's piety and virtue, as well as his military prowess: Moses is described as "an excellent general, an extremely prudent adviser, and a most reliable guardian of every person" (*Ap.* 2.17).[2] The military aspect of Moses's character is foregrounded in Josephus's retelling of the Exodus story. He relates that, before the Exodus proper, Moses had fought for Egypt against the Ethiopians—a story that is also found in the writings of the second-century BCE Alexandrian Jewish historian Artapanus. In line with the rhetoric of classical works, Josephus has Moses deliver a rousing speech to the Israelites just before the encounter with the Egyptians at the sea. Josephus even draws a direct parallel between Moses and Alexander the Great, each of whom is said to have crossed dry-shod through a body of water. Among the Hellenistic virtues that Josephus ascribes to Moses is that of temperance: Moses is said to have had "command of his passions." This stoicism might seem at odds with the biblical narrative, in which Moses famously loses his temper when confronted with the golden calf. Josephus simply omits the episode entirely, for the benefit of the reputation of both the Israelites and of Moses.

Josephus also styles Moses as a philosopher of the highest order, arguing that famous Greek philosophers, including Plato himself, learned much from Moses and his example. Similarly, Moses is noteworthy in Josephus for being a lawgiver, and thus stands in the long line of such celebrated figures in Greek history as Pericles, Lycurgus, and Solon. In all of these ways, Josephus is reconfiguring the Exodus story to make Moses more recognizable to his Hellenistic audience. Rather than being a charlatan, Moses becomes the very embodiment of classical virtues, the predecessor, and even model, for the heroes of Greek culture.

A century before Josephus, the Jewish writer Philo of Alexandria wrote a biography of Moses that also sought to translate the biblical story into a Hellenistic idiom.[3] Philo's *Life of Moses* belongs to a common Greco-Roman literary genre known as an aretology: a work intended to praise the virtue (*arete*) of the subject, and in so doing to provide a model for contemporary behavior. While Philo is best known for his allegorical interpretations of the Bible, those play little part in his biography of Moses. He uses the Exodus story not to provide his fellow Jews with deeper insight into their own tradition but to explain that tradition to a non-Jewish audience who, as we have seen, had their own less-than-glorious versions of the story. Philo states quite plainly that "the historians who have flourished among the Greeks have not chosen to think him worthy of mention" (*Mos.* 1.2). It is to remedy this that Philo undertakes his task.

Philo presents Moses as the Platonic ideal of a philosopher-king. In Midian, before returning to Egypt to free the Israelites, Moses was passing the time, according to Philo, by applying himself "to the contemplation and practice of virtue and to the continual study of the doctrines of philosophy, which he easily and thoroughly comprehended in his soul" (*Mos.* 1.48). This was also when he trained for kingship, as Philo describes Moses's leadership of the Israelites: "the business of a shepherd is preparation for the office of a king" (*Mos.* 1.60). As the philosopher-king, Moses possessed all of the classical virtues outlined by Plato and central to the writings of those philosophers who followed him: wisdom, courage, temperance, justice, and piety. In describing Moses as a philosopher-king, Philo elevated the hero of the Exodus account to one of the pinnacles of the classical world. But Philo then went on to lift Moses to further heights: not only philosopher and king, but also legislator, priest, and prophet—roles that were usually separate, and separately valued, in classical culture, but that were, miraculously, combined in the single person of Moses.

In both Josephus and Philo, the appeal to Moses as the personification of the Hellenistic world's highest virtues serves not only to push back against scurrilous descriptions of the biblical hero but also to situate the Jews more squarely in their Hellenistic environment. (Thus, even the departure from Egypt is reconceived in terms that the non-Jewish audience can understand: Philo describes the Exodus not as a hasty departure from oppression but as a colonization of Canaan—again depicting the ancient Israelites as analogous to the Greco-Roman imperial state.) These authors use the Exodus story as the font of Jewish identity, and Moses as the ideal Jew. There is something assimilationist about their positions, but not in the usual way: rather than exhorting the Jews to be more Hellenistic, Philo and Josephus attempt to convince their pagan audience to recognize the inherently Hellenistic values already present in Judaism, embodied by the founding figure of Moses.

Both of these authors also make an interesting choice in their retellings of the Exodus story: neither mentions the covenant between God and Israel at Sinai. Though both certainly grapple with the laws, as we will see presently, the concept of covenant, so central to biblical thought, is nowhere to be found. The Sinai event is practically unmentioned by Philo. This glaring omission contributes to the trend toward Hellenistic cultural assimilation that we have already observed. The Jews are not bound by an exclusive covenantal relationship with God; they may have different practices, but they are not a people apart in any existential sense. In this way these authors may also be pointing to a more universalizing notion. Instead of portraying the Jews as part of Hellenistic culture, here they suggest that their non-Jewish contemporaries could see themselves as participating in a broader covenant to which the Jews already adhere.

At the same time, however, there was no denying that it was the laws—whether specifically linked to Sinai or not—that most definitively set the Jews apart from their cultural context. For many ancient authors, both Jewish and pagan, it was Moses's role as lawgiver that was most prominent, and most controversial. There was an ongoing debate over whether Moses merely transcribed laws authored by God, or whether Moses himself was the author of the biblical legislation— with positive and negative views adhering to each position. For the most part, however, the status of lawgiver was an exalted one in Greco-Roman tradition. Even those authors who denigrated the Jews or the Exodus story still considered at least this aspect of Moses's persona to be generally positive.

Any objections were usually aimed not at the fact of Moses's lawgiving but at the nature of the laws themselves. As has almost always been the case, the regulations that keep Jews separate from their neighbors—circumcision, dietary restrictions, and strict purity laws—were viewed in the ancient world as threatening to the dominant social order. The Greek historian Hecataeus described Jewish customs as "unsocial and intolerant," a charge that has echoed through the halls of history. For some critics, however, the difficulties they saw in Jewish practices were due not to Moses but to the generations of Jews since Sinai, who had altered and updated the biblical legislation.

Philo, in the first century BCE, countered the last of these charges directly: the Jews "have not changed a single word of what he [Moses] wrote but would even endure to die a thousand deaths sooner than accept anything contrary to the laws and customs which he had ordained" (*Mos.* 2.17). Philo held up Moses as the greatest of all lawgivers: unlike the successive legislations of the Greeks and Romans, the Mosaic law had remained perfectly stable since it was given—one lawgiver, and one law, for eternity. Linked to this is the notion that, though divine inspiration is certainly not to be ruled out, Moses may well have devised the biblical laws on the basis of his own logical reasoning. Here again we can see how Philo took Greco-Roman virtues and applied them to Moses—indeed, even placing Moses at the pinnacle of those virtues, as Moses's reasoning had lasted longer than anyone else's. Eventually, said Philo, the pagan world would recognize that the laws of Moses are superior.

In some of his voluminous writings on the Bible, Philo attempts to make the biblical laws comprehensible in a strictly logical fashion. Perhaps he is aware that, unlike the law codes of his pagan contemporaries, the biblical legal materials can seem disorganized, repetitive, even contradictory at times, and generally unsystematic in nature. Thus, in his works *On the Decalogue* and *On the Special Laws*, Philo takes the laws of the Decalogue as his guiding principles and proceeds to align the rest of the biblical legislation under the general headings of the Ten Commandments. As the Ten Commandments are certainly more accessible and relatable than, say, the purity laws of Leviticus, Philo may well have arranged the text this way in order to demonstrate—to

Jews and pagans alike—that the entirety of the Jewish law speaks to a set of common values.

Philo is perhaps best known, however, for his allegorical treatment of the biblical legislation, found in works such as the *Exposition of the Laws of Moses*. As he worked through the individual laws, he provided both a literal and an allegorical reading: the surface meaning and a deeper one, heavily influenced by Greek philosophical traditions, especially Stoicism. The laws, for Philo, existed in order to guide the reader toward the proper and virtuous way of life; they were as much ethical as they were practical—and they existed not only to be obeyed but to be studied and pondered, with the aim of living "the contemplative life," as one of his books is titled. Whether or not it was intended to do so, Philo's allegorical approach to the laws assimilated the uniqueness of Jewish customs to broader classical worldviews, potentially giving them a more positive cultural standing in his Greek context. It is perhaps no surprise that Jewish tradition effectively ignored Philo, while his understanding of the law was eagerly taken up in early Christianity.

In his *Antiquities*, Josephus is more direct in his defense of the Jewish laws. Responding forcefully to those who described Moses as a charlatan, as a deceiver of his people, Josephus declares Moses to have been the preeminent lawgiver, and the laws themselves to have been a gift from God to the Jewish people: they are "rules for a blissful life and an ordered government" (*Ant.* 3.84). In his polemical work *Against Apion*, devoted to a rebuttal of the anti-Jewish author Apion, Josephus sets the laws of Moses higher than those of even the great Greek lawgivers, not only for their own inherent virtues, but, presciently, because adherence to the laws provides the Jews with a common bond, one that can sustain them even through periods of persecution. Josephus's final words in *Against Apion* are worth presenting in full here:

> A glance at [the laws] showed that they teach not impiety, but the most genuine piety; that they invite men not to hate their fellows, but to share their possessions; that they are the foes of injustice and scrupulous for justice, banish sloth and extravagance, and teach men to be self-dependent and to work with a will; that they deter them from war for the sake of conquest, but render them valiant defenders of the laws themselves; inexorable in punishment, not to be duped by studied words, always supported by actions. For actions are our invariable testimonials, plainer than any documents. I would therefore boldly maintain that we have introduced to the rest of the world a very large number of very beautiful ideas. What higher justice than obedience to the laws?

At once a defense of the Jewish laws and a recasting of them in solid classical values—piety, justice, work ethic, modesty, independence—this passage illustrates how ancient Jewish authors living in the Greco-Roman cultural context were forced to play both sides, as it were. Regardless of how the laws were understood, the fact remains that both Philo and Josephus, and others as well, felt a need to render them less inscrutable, both to counter the scurrilous attacks of pagan critics and, equally, to maintain their relevance for the Jewish communities constantly buffeted by the overwhelming forces of Hellenism. The laws set the Jews apart, in their own eyes and in those of their neighbors—but they could also be recast to show that the Jews were in line with the values of those peoples among whom they lived.

Exodus in the New Testament

The prominence of the Exodus story in the New Testament should come as no surprise. The era of the New Testament, that is, essentially the first century CE, is coterminous with the period of the noncanonical Jewish writings that we have just discussed. Indeed, the New Testament is itself nothing other than a Greco-Roman Jewish text: its authors would have considered themselves to be Jewish, at least insofar as Jesus himself was Jewish. Even as Jesus's followers struck a new course, eventuating in a different religion altogether, in its earliest decades Christianity was simply another sect of Judaism, alongside the Pharisees, Sadducees, Zealots, and others.

Much of the New Testament is also addressed to Jews, either explicitly or implicitly. Thus, it would have been entirely sensible for its authors, in trying to bring the audience to follow Jesus, to hearken back to the long-established central tradition of the Hebrew Bible, to the story that had come to define Judaism. If the Jews were, at heart, the people of the Exodus, then it was imperative to bring that story to bear on the Jesus movement as well. Far easier—and more rhetorically effective—to show Jewish contemporaries that the new movement was part of the continuing narrative than to mark it as a complete and total break with the past. As the New Testament scholar Dale Allison has written, "A Jesus fundamentally discontinuous with the Jewish tradition could not have been Israel's Messiah, for the latter was a feature of the former."[4]

The cultural context of Roman imperial power, so central to the readings of Exodus by Josephus, played a significant role in the adaptation of the Exodus story by the New Testament authors. New social organizations were viewed with suspicion in the Roman Empire, as early Christians quickly learned; association with an established group, even a culturally subordinate one, was politically savvy. Moreover, for followers of the Jesus movement, it was possible to see an important parallel with the ancient narrative. Just as Moses inaugurated a new set of religious practices and beliefs, so too Jesus, in the new Egypt of imperial Rome, was offering a new beginning, a new covenant, for a new era of Judaism.

The concept of the "new covenant," established through the blood of Jesus at the Last Supper, is central in the texts of the New Testament. "This is my blood of the covenant," says Jesus in Mark 14:24; in Luke 22:20, "This cup that is poured out for you is the new covenant in my blood." Though the Hebrew Bible contains numerous covenants, going back to Abraham, the reference to the blood in these passages looks more directly at the covenant ceremony of Exodus 24, after the giving of the Ten Commandments and the laws of Exodus 21–23, when Moses proclaims, "Behold the blood of the covenant" (Exod 24:8).[5] The twelve disciples to whom Jesus speaks stand in for the twelve tribes addressed by Moses. In the New Testament epistles, the new covenant of Jesus is understood as a fulfillment of Jeremiah's prophecy, "The days are coming, says Yahweh, when I will make a new covenant with the house of Israel and the house of Judah" (Jer 31:31). (There is also a clear connection between Jesus offering his blood and body for the sake of his followers and the sacrificial Passover offering, but this will be discussed further in chapter 4.)

In drawing directly on this seminal moment in the Exodus story, the New Testament authors—if not in fact Jesus himself—cleverly articulate both a sense of continuity and a sense of a new beginning. The language is recognizable; the concept is familiar; those who heard it would immediately understand themselves to be participating in a tradition that tied them back to their ancestors, standing at Sinai witnessing the word of God. (Note that just before Moses announces the blood of the covenant, the people of Israel have all unanimously acclaimed, "All that Yahweh has spoken we will do, and we will be obedient.") Yet this was not the usual way in which a Jewish audience encountered these words, which would have been in the liturgical reading of the biblical text or in the course of traditional study. Here they appeared in a new proclamation for a new Israel, with new conditions under a new covenant.

It is in the Gospel of Matthew that the connections to the Exodus story are deepest and broadest.[6] As Matthew is often understood to be the most Jewish of the gospel writers, this is hardly unexpected. A century ago, the scholar Benjamin W. Bacon argued that the structure of Matthew mirrors that of the Pentateuch, and can be divided into five sections paralleling the five books of Moses. More recent scholarship, particularly that of Dale Allison, has focused on Matthew's thoroughgoing presentation of Jesus as a new Moses. Allison usefully presents the parallel structure in the form of a chart:[7]

Matthew	The Pentateuch	
1–2	Exod 1:1–2:10	infancy narrative
3:13–17	Exod 14:10–31	crossing of water
4:1–11	Exod 16:1–17:7	wilderness temptation
5–7	Exod 19:1–23:33	mountain of lawgiving
11:25–30	Exod 33:1–23	reciprocal knowledge of God
17:1–9	Exod 34:29–35	transfiguration
28:16–20	Deut 31:7–9	commissioning of successor
	Josh 1:1–9	

Some of these parallels go beyond mere structure: in Matthew 17:3 (and in Mark 9:4 and Luke 9:30 as well), Jesus ascends a mountain where he actually meets Moses (and Elijah), putting Jesus on a conceptual and even physical par with Israel's greatest prophets.

Though there is hardly space here to discuss every similarity between the Exodus story of Moses and the story of Jesus in the Gospel of Matthew, it may suffice to address one in particular, that is, the opening episodes of each. Just as the Exodus story begins with the famous tale of the birth of Moses, so too Matthew begins with the birth of Jesus. (Compare the earliest of the gospels, Mark, which opens with Jesus's adult baptism by John.) In Exodus, Moses's birth is set in the context of Pharaoh's command that every male child born to an Israelite should be killed; in Matthew, Herod's command to slaughter every child under the age of two born in Bethlehem is a response to the announcement of Jesus's birth.

The direct connection between Jesus and Moses is solidified in the descent of Jesus and his family to Egypt: "An angel of the Lord appeared to Joseph in a dream and said, 'Get up, take the child and his mother, and flee to Egypt, and remain there until I tell you, for Herod is about to search for the child, to destroy him'" (Matt 2:13). The parallel with Moses's fleeing from Pharaoh is undeniable: "When Pharaoh learned of the matter, he sought to kill Moses; but Moses fled from Pharaoh" (Exod 2:15). Whereas Moses flees from Egypt, Jesus and his family escape to it. This effectively accomplishes two goals for the gospel writer: it directly links Jesus to Egypt, thereby placing him in the precise context of the Exodus tradition; and at the same time, it smartly identifies Herod with Pharaoh, and the Roman Empire with the kingdom of Egypt. The new Exodus of Matthew reorients the reader for the new revelation to come.

This reorientation plays with the same notions of communal identity that we have already encountered both in the Hebrew Bible and in the early postbiblical Jewish writings. As Allison puts it, "By uniting themselves to their Scripturally faithful Mosaic Lord, Christians were uniting themselves to the sacred past of the Jews, the one people of God: to belong to Jesus Christ was to belong to Israel's history and so to have her memories."[8] Through this process the Hebrew Bible was taken up into Christianity as a fundamental text rather than as an obsolete remnant of the past. The Exodus story provided the link, the fulcrum, for the transition from one communal identity to another.

In a number of early Jewish interpretive texts, Moses is treated not only as Israel's first great prophet and leader but also as the ultimate model for all subsequent such figures. In particular, there was much focus on Moses as the intermediary between God and Israel, as the one who received laws and truths normally hidden from humanity, and as the one who stood in the breach to bring about reconciliation when God was angry with Israel. In the Gospel of John, these themes are taken up and redirected toward Jesus, who dons the mantle of prophetic leadership in the style of Moses.[9]

John, unlike Matthew, does not feel beholden to the strictures of Jewish law. Yet, like Matthew, John still recognizes the need to align the teachings of Jesus with those of Moses. "The law was given through Moses; grace and truth came through Jesus Christ" (John 1:17). In place of the laws, Jesus offers love: "I give you a new commandment, that you love one another" (John 13:34). Not an equation but a parallel is drawn here and elsewhere in the gospel. The teachings of Jesus are put on a level playing field with those of Moses, the rhetorical argument being that obedience to the latter ought to now be transformed into obedience to the former. "If you believed Moses, you would believe me, for he wrote about me. But if you do not believe what he wrote, how will you believe what I say?," Jesus asks the Jews (John 5:46–47). Jesus is both the equivalent and the fulfillment of Moses.

John elevates Jesus by comparing him explicitly with Moses: "it was not Moses who gave you the bread from heaven, but it is my Father who gives you the true bread from heaven" (John 6:32). The intercessory role for which Moses had been acclaimed is effectively rejected here, replaced not only by God but by Jesus himself, who is the bread from heaven. "Your ancestors ate the manna in the wilderness, and they died . . . I am the living bread that came down from heaven. Whoever eats of this bread will live forever" (John 6:49, 51). Similarly, John directly takes on the Jewish tradition that Moses had ascended to heaven when he received the laws at Mount Sinai: "No one has ascended into heaven except he who descended from heaven, the Son of Man" (John 3:13).

The most fascinating aspect of John's use of Exodus themes, particularly his attention to the figure of Moses, is that they appear to be a response not to the pressure of Roman imperial culture, as was the case with Josephus and Matthew, but rather to the traditions of a deeply skeptical contemporaneous Judaism. As Wayne Meeks put it, "Substantial portions of the Johannine tradition were shaped by a fluid situation of missionary and polemical interaction with a strong Jewish community."[10] Meeks points out that John's putative opponents in the gospel, in John 5 and 9, contest Jesus's divinity on the grounds that he does not respect the Sabbath, and it is in response to this challenge that Jesus sets himself over and against Moses. The message of John is not that the Exodus traditions have been abrogated by Jesus, but that they have been superseded. His audience is called to move beyond the traditional Exodus story, to stop clinging to an outdated (Jewish) mode of revelation, and to come to the new revelation of Jesus—itself, despite the polemic, still fundamentally grounded in the Exodus story.

In his letter to the Corinthians, Paul treads an interesting middle ground with respect to the Exodus story.[11] He is writing predominantly to Gentiles, so one may ask why he feels the need to make references to the paradigmatic Jewish narrative at all. As we have seen, however, the broader Greco-Roman world was not unfamiliar with the Exodus story, though they may have often employed it as anti-Jewish polemic. Perhaps more to the point, the persistent presence of Jews living among the Gentile communities may have stood as proof that there was power to be drawn from their experience and traditions. As the community of Jesus followers was being asked to take up a similarly isolated position within the broader pagan culture, both the continuing existence of the Jews and the devotion they showed to their traditions could be taken as models to emulate.

For Paul, then, the call to the Corinthians is not to become Jewish but rather to recognize that Jesus had brought about a new kind of Exodus for his followers. This is accomplished by aligning Jesus with the fundamental moment of the Exodus story: the Passover sacrifice. In 1 Corinthians 5, Paul claims, "Our paschal lamb, Christ, has been sacrificed" (5:7). This statement comes about in the course of castigating the Corinthians for sexual immorality, which Paul describes metaphorically, using a common saying: "A little yeast leavens the whole batch of dough." The sin is the leaven. And just as the Israelites removed their leaven before the Passover sacrifice, so too the Corinthians should be free from sin when Christ is sacrificed.

Later, in chapter 10, where Paul explicitly compares Christian baptism to the crossing of the Red Sea, he returns to the same theme: the sins of the Corinthians are like those of the Israelites in the wilderness. Though God provided for his people as they crossed the desert, they were nevertheless disobedient, and died for it. God has now provided for his people again, by sending Christ—"They drank from the spiritual rock that followed them, and the rock was Christ" (1 Cor 10:4)—and so now there is a new opportunity placed before all, to do better than the Israelites did. "These things occurred as examples for us, so that we might not desire evil as they did" (1 Cor 10:6).

The Exodus story for Paul may contain elements of typology, as in Matthew, and a degree of supersession, as in John. It was, however, primarily a historical lesson to learn from, as it was essentially happening again, right in Paul's present. For Paul the focus on morality and behavior was especially pressing, as he believed that Jesus signaled the imminent advent of the end times. The historical salvation of the Israelites was being played out now, as, and at, the end of history. A complete cleansing was thus necessary, in order that Christ's followers might "celebrate the festival, not with the old yeast, the yeast of malice and evil, but with the unleavened bread of sincerity and truth" (1 Cor 5:8).

Conclusion

In the Hebrew Bible and early postbiblical Jewish interpretation, the Exodus story's power lay not just in its recording of Israel's past but in its fundamental status as the defining narrative of Israelite and Jewish identity for the authors' contemporaneous present(s). All those who considered themselves to be part of the people of Israel were implicated in the story. Just as the Jewish people were called to think of themselves as having stood at Sinai, so too they could understand themselves to be eternally participating in the Exodus. For the authors of the New Testament, this tradition was largely maintained, though with a new twist. Israel was being redefined as those who followed Jesus, and the Exodus was not merely a moment in history to be relived but a moment in the present to be experienced directly.

Across these treatments from the biblical period, a few regular themes emerge as common. In both the Hebrew Bible and in the New Testament, the Passover sacrifice stands as central, manifested in the regular commemoration of the Exodus event through the observance of Passover, or through the recognition of Jesus as the new paschal offering. The figure of Moses, especially in his role as lawgiver, reached new heights in early postbiblical Jewish writings, and became a topic of contestation in the New Testament: What constituted the ultimate revelation—Moses's laws or the new way inaugurated by Jesus? For the communities of Jews and Jesus followers living under Greco-Roman imperial rule, the Exodus story offered an obvious model both for divine protection and salvation, and for the formation of a distinctive and long-lasting communal identity.

In short, many, if not all, of the later uses to which the Exodus tradition would be put were already very much present in the earliest treatments of the story, even those that are found in the Bible itself. Though the events of the story were not up for debate, its meaning was constantly contested, adapted, and updated for the needs of each community, and indeed each individual author.

FIG. 3: Illuminated page from the Barcelona Haggadah (BL Add MS 14761 fol. 30v). Photo courtesy of the British Library.

Exodus as Ritual

If there was a historical Exodus (see chapter 1 for the "if"), it happened exactly once in Israel's history, in the time of Moses, more than three millennia ago. Yet it is reexperienced every year, and perhaps even more often than that, down to the present. The Exodus may be the oldest historical event to be continually memorialized in Western tradition, with a good thousand-year head start over Hanukkah or Christmas. It has retained its position not merely because it is a good story—there are many good stories from the ancient world, many of which predate the Exodus—but because, from the very beginning, it was ritualized: represented not only in the retelling of the story but in actions, in dietary regulations, and in an annually performed script. The Exodus story lives on by having been codified in behavior. And that behavior, in turn, reinforces both the story itself and the communal identity of the groups that participate in it.

Rituals are both conservative and progressive. On the one hand, they naturally resist change. Their meaning resides in the repetition of their performance, often to the point that the original concepts underlying the ritual acts have been forgotten—at which point the performance of the ritual makes its own meaning, at least in terms of identity formation. On the other hand, no ritual remains static

forever; as time passes and cultures change and develop, rituals are subtly—and sometimes not so subtly—adapted to
meet contemporary needs.

In this chapter we will explore the origins and developments of the ritualized Exodus story, from its beginnings in
the Hebrew Bible through the creation and growth of the
Jewish Passover Seder and Haggadah, and to the quite different Christian adoption of the Passover ritual in the Lord's
Supper, or Eucharist, and the celebration of Easter. Though
each stage has its distinctive elements, they share a common
basis in the Exodus story, and a common result: the tying
together of a community via history, tradition, and story,
wrapped in a ritual package.

The Passover Ritual in the Hebrew Bible

Originally, as noted in chapter 2, the celebrations of the
pesah and the seven-day festival of unleavened bread were
not connected to the Exodus story: they were recognitions
of God's continuing protection of the Israelites and an agricultural festival, respectively. Yet on the literary level, within
the text of the Bible itself, there is no doubt that these communal events were understood as celebrations of God's rescue of the Israelites from Egypt.

Although the first place we encounter the rituals of Passover is in the book of Exodus, the earliest writing that institutes a ritual celebration of the Exodus is in the book of Deuteronomy, in the festival legislation of Deuteronomy 16.
Here we read, "Observe the month of Abib and offer a passover sacrifice to Yahweh your God, for it was in the month of

Abib, at night, that Yahweh your God freed you from Egypt" (16:1). This was most likely the first time that anyone had linked the long-standing pesah sacrifice with the departure from Egypt. This sacrificial offering, like all sacrifices, was to be held at the temple in Jerusalem, where its meat was to be cooked and eaten; the next day everyone was to return home, where they were instructed to avoid eating anything leavened for the next seven days: "for seven days thereafter you shall eat unleavened bread, bread of distress—for you departed from the land of Egypt hurriedly—so that you remember the day of your departure from Egypt as long as you live" (16:3). In this legislation, we can see the two originally separate rituals of pesah and unleavened bread being combined, not only calendrically but also conceptually: both are understood as commemoration of the Exodus.

The earliest version of the biblical text of Exodus contained no such ritual legislation. The story in Exodus, as discussed in chapter 1, is an amalgam of originally independent narrative threads. The J and P sources, most prominent in the description of the departure from Egypt, make no statements whatsoever about future observance; they simply narrate the onetime events that occurred in Egypt. For both, this included the death of the Egyptian firstborn. For J, however, there is also the element of haste, to which we owe the tradition of the unleavened bread that the Israelites took with them as they fled by night. For P, by contrast, the departure was not hasty at all: the Israelites walked out in broad daylight. P, however, provided us with the slaughter of a lamb and the daubing of its blood on the doorposts and lintels of the Israelite houses so that God would know not to kill the firstborn within.

At some later point—after the P story had been written, but before it had been combined with that of J—a later priestly editor, aware of the festival legislation in Deuteronomy, added similar ritual material to the account in what is now Exodus 12. "This day shall be to you one of remembrance: you shall celebrate it as a festival to Yahweh throughout the ages; you shall celebrate it as an institution for all time" (Exod 12:14). With this, a onetime historical event was transformed into an annual commemoration. And although the P narrative makes no mention of unleavened bread in the context of the departure from Egypt, this later editor, in light of the connection already made in Deuteronomy, makes sure to cement the link between the two: "You shall observe the feast of unleavened bread, for on this very day I brought your ranks out of the land of Egypt; you shall observe this day throughout the ages as an institution for all time" (12:17). This later stratum of the text goes on to provide laws regarding the Passover sacrifice that are explicitly and exclusively relevant for future generations, for those who have long since settled in the promised land: "No foreigner may eat of it. . . . If a stranger who dwells with you would offer the passover to Yahweh, all his males must be circumcised" (12:43, 48). The presence of non-Israelites in the community is hardly sensible in the context of the original Exodus event; it is only once the Israelites have their own territory that a stranger can dwell with them.

In subsequent biblical texts, probably from the same editorial stratum identifiable in Exodus 12, the Passover and unleavened bread celebrations are placed firmly in the official festival calendar: "In the first month, on the fourteenth day of the month, at twilight, there shall be a passover offering to Yahweh, and on the fifteenth day of that month Yahweh's Feast of Unleavened Bread. You shall eat unleavened bread for seven days" (Lev 23:5–6). With this, the move from historical event to ongoing annual celebration was completed, and the original purposes of the pesah and unleavened bread rituals entirely effaced, replaced by a now single, multipart commemoration of the Exodus.

This move had two significant consequences. First, the inclusion of forward-looking ritual legislation in the telling of the Exodus story itself—"throughout the ages as an institution for all time"—resulted in the narrative itself being inextricable from the ritual practices attached to it. Although other stories in the Bible would come to be associated with communal festivals—the giving of the law at Sinai, for instance, would be commemorated at the spring festival of Shavuot—those connections are always made outside the story itself, and sometimes even outside the Bible altogether. Not so with the Exodus story: for more than 2,500 years, it has been, quite simply, impossible to read this story without also encountering the ritualization of it.

Second, the transformation of a protective sacrifice and, more importantly, an agricultural festival into a historical commemoration contributed significantly to the communal formation of the Israelite, and eventually Jewish, people. Although it is safe to say that the vast majority of ancient Israelites were agriculturalists, there were, of course, some who were not: merchants, scribes, priests, government officials, and others. And even among those who were primarily farmers, the early agricultural festivals were not tied to a specific calendrical date: they would be celebrated at the appropriate moment in the yearly cycle of sowing and harvesting, which would differ from region to region. With the historicization of these rituals—or the ritualization of history—the entire community, regardless of geographical or social location, participated simultaneously and identically, at least in theory.

A remarkable early example of this survives from fifth-century BCE Egypt, from a military garrison on the Nile known as Elephantine (modern-day Aswan), where a community of Israelites had lived since the seventh century BCE, isolated from the practices and beliefs of Israel proper. In 419 BCE, a papyrus was written that, though only partially preserved, still clearly contains instructions for the practice of the seven-day Passover celebration. The prohibition on eating leaven is mentioned, and perhaps even more remarkably, the precise dates of the observance: from the fifteenth through the twenty-first of Nisan, the same dates mentioned in the Bible.[1] Despite their distance from the center of the Israelite nation, the community at Elephantine joined with their fellow Israelites in observing Passover at the appropriate time.

Collective ritual led to a stronger collective identity, as can still be seen today: when every Jewish person around the world sits down to the Passover Seder on the same day every year, a sense of connection and belonging is created, linking what are otherwise enormously diverse populations.

The Jewish Passover Seder

In the period before the Roman destruction of the Second Temple in Jerusalem in 70 CE, the Passover sacrifice seems to have been offered annually, and largely in conformity with the biblical instructions. Multiple sources from around that time describe the ritual, in varying detail: Philo, Josephus, and, most prominently, the Mishnah, the compilation of Jewish laws produced in the second century CE.[2] That the sources from this period focus their attention on the pesah sacrifice, rather than on the festival of unleavened bread, is understandable when it is remembered that in the biblical period, it was the first night, when the pesah sacrifice was offered, that required intensive ritual actions. The slaughter of the animal, the placing of its blood, the timing of the offering, the other items that were required to make the sacrifice efficacious, the preparation of the meat, where it was to be eaten, the manner of the disposal of its remains— all of these were dictated by the ritual laws. For the seven days that followed, by contrast, virtually the only instruction was that there was to be no leaven found in any house, and none consumed. The private dietary practices of the faithful were of less importance, or at least required less detailed explanation, than the public sacrifice and consumption of the Passover offering. The weight of the communal practice thus fell disproportionately on the first night, on the pesah.

The destruction of the Second Temple, however, required a radical change in virtually every aspect of Jewish religious practice, if Judaism were to survive the loss of its central shrine. This was the fundamental reconfiguration brought about by the early rabbis, the creation of something much like the Judaism that we still recognize today. A new non-temple form of Judaism would also entail a serious reconsideration of how the Exodus was commemorated on Passover. With no possibility of sacrifice, how was the Jewish community to celebrate this most important festival?[3]

The biblical narrative of the Exodus already provided part of a solution. Although the formal pesah offering had to be made at the temple, as all sacrifices were, the story of the first Passover in Egypt, before the temple was built, situated the ritual practices in the individual homes of the Israelites, where they were protected from the plague of the firstborn. Thus, the relocation of the Passover ceremony from the public courtyard to the private house was not as drastic as it might have been. Similarly, while all sacrifices were offered by cultic officials (the priests) when the temple stood, in the biblical story it was the Israelites who selected, slaughtered, and consumed the pesah in Egypt. In the new post-temple era, the priests, having been put out of a job, were replaced by the laity, who would lead and participate in the Passover service, just as it was the common Israelite who placed the blood on his lintels and doorposts in Egypt.

The pesah ritual involved the consumption of the offering by the Israelites. So it was clear enough that the post-temple ceremony should also, indeed primarily, involve a meal. But in the absence of the sacrifice, what was to be eaten? The biblical legislation demanded that the offering be consumed along with bitter herbs and unleavened bread. In the Passover Seder, these retained their required status, with the added suggestion to consume haroset (the mixture meant to represent the bricks that the Israelites made for Pharaoh). In this manner, what had originally been essentially side dishes, contingent on the consumption of the main dish sacrificial offering, moved to the center of the ceremonial meal, making up for the absence of the pesah itself.

Though some aspects of the new Passover protocol could be borrowed from the narrative of the first Passover as described in the Bible, others were transformations of what had been temple rituals to the home setting. Just as the rabbis instituted the thrice-daily prayer service to replace the three daily sacrificial offerings in the temple, they now linked the Seder, the ceremonial Passover meal, to the now-defunct pesah offering. In the Mishnah, it is ruled that the Seder should begin at the same time that the pesah sacrifice had been offered: just as the pesah was offered "in the evening, at sundown" (Deut 16:6), so too "on the eve of Passover, close to the time of *minha* [the early evening service], a person should not eat until it gets dark" (*m. Pes.* 10:1).

Today, the biblical psalms are understood most often as the basis for personal expressions of faith, as manifestations of the human condition, in all its variety, from praise and thanksgiving to lament and mourning. In the biblical period, however, they were the liturgy of the temple cultus: the book of Chronicles describes David instituting the formal singing of the psalms to accompany the temple rituals. (At least formally, this remains the case today: the psalms constitute a significant part of the liturgy in both Jewish and Christian houses of worship.) In the Mishnah, the rabbis determined that a set of psalms of praise, Psalms 113–19, should be recited at the Passover Seder. It is possible that these were the very psalms that were performed during the pesah ritual when the temple still stood; in any case, the institution of this liturgy during the Passover Seder was yet another mechanism for bringing the temple service into the home. Now, however, no official singers were required. The roles of the clergy were taken up by the laity.

Perhaps the best-known aspect of the Passover Seder—at least the one that feels most approachable to an outsider—is the practice of encouraging the children present to ask about the meanings of the rituals and other symbolic elements, and the requirement to retell the story of the Exodus. The inquiry of the children has biblical roots: "When your children ask you, 'What do you mean by this rite?,' you shall say, 'It is the passover sacrifice to Yahweh, because he passed over the houses of the Israelites in Egypt when he smote the Egyptians, but saved our houses'" (Exod 12:26–27). In the Bible, this question is linked to the performance of the pesah sacrifice. In the absence of the temple, the Mishnah generalizes the question to be about the entire experience of the Seder, this most unusual of meals: "Here the son asks his father—and if the son has not enough understanding, his father instructs him how to ask—'Why is this night different from all other nights?'" (*m. Pes.* 10:4). This is the beginning of the famous Four Questions, traditionally asked by the youngest child at the table. By replacing the sacrifice with the Seder as the object of the inquiry, the Mishnah reinforces the perception that this home ritual has become the equivalent of the obsolete sacrificial ritual.

The answer to the Four Questions, according to the Mishnah, is the rehearsal of the biblical story, "from the disgrace to the glory"—that is, from the descent into Egypt until the deliverance from Egypt. This telling of the story is not merely a part of the Seder, it is its very center and raison d'être: the script for the Seder is known as the Haggadah, literally "the telling."

The Mishnah goes on to require that the father then provide commentary on a biblical passage that was originally unconnected with the Passover festival. In Deuteronomy 26, the Israelites are commanded to bring the first fruits of their

harvest to the sanctuary every year, and upon doing so to recite an abbreviated history of their history, from "My father
was a wandering Aramean. He went down to Egypt" until
"He brought us to this place and gave us this land, a land flowing with milk and honey" (Deut 26:5–9). After the destruction of the temple and the exile of so many Jews from Israel,
however, this last verse seemed out of place, and so it was determined that the passage invoked at the Seder should end
one verse earlier, appropriately enough with "Yahweh freed us
from Egypt by a mighty hand, by an outstretched arm and
awesome power, and by signs and portents." Having just told
the story of the Exodus, this brief précis of the narrative might
seem unnecessary. The key here, however, is that the verses
from Deuteronomy are not simply to be recited at the Seder,
but they are to be expounded upon, that is, explored for
meanings deeper than those apparent from a surface reading.
This practice, known as midrash, brings the fixed text of the
past to life, to bear on the present. For the Jews living shortly
after the destruction of the temple and the collapse of their
entire previous way of life, the Exodus story had, as we have
already seen, enormous potential to provide hope in a time of
darkness. And by selecting for interpretation a text that was
intended by the biblical authors to unite the Israelite community in a common appreciation of God's blessings on them,
the Mishnah does the same for the dispersed Jewish community. Though they may not be settled in their land, capable of
offering their first fruits at the temple, they could, in recalling
the past redemption of their ancestors, maintain hope for
their own redemption in the future—and the hope that they
could one day again declare, "He brought us to this place and
gave us this land, a land flowing with milk and honey."

Beyond telling the story and expounding the biblical verses, the Seder is considered incomplete unless one has explained the meaning of the three central elements: "Passover, unleavened bread, and bitter herbs. Passover—because God passed over the houses of our fathers in Egypt; unleavened bread—because our fathers were redeemed from Egypt; bitter herbs—because the Egyptians embittered the lives of our fathers in Egypt" (*m. Pes.* 10:5). Rituals are often opaque, their original meaning lost in the passage of time or subsumed by the very act of performing them, uniting its practitioners in common behavior. The Seder, however, brings the explicit explanation of the rituals to the forefront, ensuring that their meaning cannot be lost: this ceremony is grounded in God's redemption of Israel. (Note that, in this way, the Seder cannot be recontextualized, as, ironically, the agricultural festival of unleavened bread itself had been.) Moreover, these explanations not only elucidate the ritual elements of the Seder meal but themselves become part of the newly constructed ritual.

In the questioning and storytelling at the heart of the Seder, we see a reflection of the status of the Exodus story already established in the biblical period. This is the fundamental story of Israel, and subsequently of Judaism. It is definitional: it is how Israel describes itself. Rituals bind communities together, and the ritual of the Seder is one of narrative. In order to participate, one need only feel the force of the story. The ritual retains its power regardless of place or time.

The transformation by the Mishnah of the pesah sacrifice into the Seder meal involved a series of practical changes, as outlined above. It also resulted in a number of more intangible effects, rendering the ritual more applicable to the post-temple Jewish existence and providing it with the power to endure down to the present.

As we have already seen, the newly prescribed Seder removed authority from cultic experts—priests, Levites, and official cultic singers—and bestowed it on the laity. More accurately, perhaps, it equalized authority: priests and other cultic servants are still obligated to perform the Seder, of course, but they do so in exactly the same way as the farmer, the merchant, the scribe, and everyone else. In other words, the Seder effectively flattened the social divisions that were so crucial to the Israelite cult, creating a major ritual practice that could be led, and participated in, by every Jew, everywhere. By providing a protoscript for the Seder (which would, as we will see, be expanded into a much fuller version), the Mishnah also ensured that one would need only minimal expertise, if any, to perform the ritual meal. Even the children in attendance are given an important role, one that is tailored to their level of knowledge. As the anthropologist Ruth Fredman Cernea wrote: "The structure of the Seder permits, indeed requires, each person to join the ritual whatever his or her degree of learning, belief, social status, or ritual participation at other times. 'Society' is defined in its widest sense, as opposed to many other ritual procedures in Jewish culture that exclude people because of their age or sex. All communication that takes place at the Seder must be available to everyone."[4] The Seder transformed a ritual act performed by priests on behalf of the community into a ritual performed by the community for itself.

It also gave Judaism a ritual structure independent of any central location: this fundamentally important ritual act does not even occur in a local synagogue but in the home. It thus matters not at all where one lives: whether in a close-knit urban Jewish community or in a cabin in the farthest wilderness, this signal marker of Jewish identity can be performed anywhere at all. The significance of this for contemporary Jewish life should be relatively obvious, but it was even more pressing in the immediate aftermath of the destruction of the Second Temple. Though some Jews did remain in the land of Israel, virtually none were in Jerusalem, and most, for the first time in history, were scattered among foreign lands. Thus the need to preserve cultural and communal continuity, both vertically, that is, between past and present, and horizontally, across the Jewish diaspora, was both acute and new. We take for granted, perhaps, that the expression of Jewish identity is geographically unbound; for the authors of the Mishnah, this was anything but obvious. The biblical laws are deeply tied to the land of Israel, to Jerusalem, to the temple; the most important accomplishment of the early rabbis is that they were able to create a Judaism that both maintained the necessary connection with the biblical past and made the necessary adjustments for a very different kind of future.

If the later editors of the Bible ensured that the Exodus story could not be read without having to learn about its ritualization, the Seder ensures that the ritual of Exodus cannot be experienced without having to hear the story. In encouraging questions from the children, in retelling the narrative, and in expounding biblical verses, the story is not only remembered but reexperienced, brought into contact with the present. The pesah sacrifice was an act of commemoration; the Passover Seder is an act of commiseration, and of communal redemption. The Mishnah makes this explicit: "In every generation a man must so regard himself as if he came forth himself out of Egypt, for it is written [in Exod 13:8]: 'And you shall explain to your son on that day, "It is because of what Yahweh did for me when I went free from Egypt"'" (*m. Pes.* 10:5). Participation in the Seder is participation in the Exodus itself. It is story, not history; living, not confined to the past.

In this, the Seder effectively overcomes our modern questions regarding the historicity of the Exodus (though the Mishnah surely would never have considered this a valid question). I clearly remember, early in my doctoral education, my uncle calling me on the phone to say that he had just heard someone say that the Exodus never really happened. When I confirmed that this was generally accurate, he burst out, "Then what the hell are we doing at Passover every year?" The answer is that Passover is not meant to reconfirm, annually, the historical events of the Exodus; Jews do not sit at the table and examine the textual and archaeological records of the past; they are not commemorating a moment in time. The Seder, rather, is an opportunity to place oneself in a story, to feel for oneself, with the other members of the Jewish community, what it means to be oppressed, and to be redeemed from that oppression. It is an empathetic ritual. The story—not history, but living story—is shared with every Jew around the world, and with all those from previous generations who have participated in the same empathetic process.

The Seder was established in the Mishnah at the end of the second century CE, but it was not frozen in form. The rabbis of the Talmud, the commentary on the Mishnah produced over the following three to four hundred years, continued to expand the Seder program, and expound further on its constituent elements. Included in this expansion are such set pieces as the Four Children, which takes as its starting point the four times in the Bible that parents are instructed to explain Israel's history to their offspring, and develops a midrash in which each question represents a different type of child: wise, wicked, simple, and too young to ask. Here again we can see the focus on involving and representing children in the ritual commemoration of the Exodus. Another midrash from this period describes four rabbis who spend all night discussing the Exodus at their Seder, such that their students have to remind them that morning has come. This addition takes up and amplifies the narrative function of the Seder. In both of these cases, the midrash in question was not invented for the purpose of inclusion in the Seder but was borrowed from an earlier collection; that is, the Exodus story and its commemoration were, unsurprisingly, generating interpretation and commentary even outside the formal Seder setting. (And there are innumerable other midrashic texts that never made it into the Seder.)

As the rabbis continued adding to the requirements of the Seder, a new literary form developed: not a series of laws, as we have in the Mishnah, but something closer to a script. This script came to be known as the Haggadah, "the telling," again emphasizing that the center of the ritual is to be found in the narration of the Exodus story and the discussion of its meaning. For instance, the leader of the Seder is to raise the matza and proclaim, "This is the bread of affliction that our ancestors ate in the land of Egypt. Whoever is hungry, let him come and eat; whoever is in need, let him come and conduct the Seder of Passover. This year we are here; next year in the land of Israel. This year we are slaves; next year free people." This declaration begins the telling of the story, and leads directly into the Four Questions (which themselves were changed over time from the original questions found in the Mishnah). After the Four Questions, another formal proclamation is to be recited: "We were slaves to Pharaoh in Egypt, and Yahweh our God took us out of there with a strong hand and with an outstretched arm. If the Holy One, blessed be He, had not taken our ancestors out of Egypt, then we, our children, and our children's children would have remained enslaved to Pharaoh in Egypt. Even if all of us were wise, all of us understanding, all of us knowing the Torah, we would still be obligated to discuss the Exodus from Egypt; and everyone who discusses the Exodus from Egypt at length is praiseworthy." It is not just the telling of the story but the discussion of it, the bringing it to bear upon the present, that is demanded here; and the social leveling that we have already seen to be present in the Seder ritual is made explicit here as well.

By the ninth century, the Haggadah had reached something very close to its final form. Rav Amram Gaon, the head of the Jewish academy in Sura, a city in modern-day Iraq, included a complete Haggadah in his prayer book, a work that formed the basis for most modern Jewish liturgies (in part because it had the support of Rashi, perhaps the greatest Jewish figure of the medieval period). The song "Dayyenu," in which thanks is given for all that God has done for the Jewish people, was already a part of Rav Amram's Haggadah, though it was not found in the Mishnah or Talmud. A few hundred years later, the great Jewish scholar

Maimonides included a Haggadah in the Mishneh Torah, his codification of Jewish law.

Over the following centuries, still further additions were made to the Haggadah. These included the singing of songs—not psalms or prayers—at the end of the meal, such as "Chad Gadya," which has no connection with the Exodus story whatsoever, but is, rather, a folk song more akin to "There was an old woman who swallowed a fly." This song is among the latest inclusions in the traditional Haggadah, appearing first at the end of the sixteenth century, though the song itself is believed to be earlier.

Among the most famous of these later supplements to the Haggadah is Elijah's cup: the cup of wine that sits on the table throughout the meal, set aside for the possibility that the prophet Elijah, the herald of the messiah, might appear to partake of it. The story of how Elijah's cup became part of the Seder exemplifies the flexible and interpretive nature of the ritual. It had been determined already in the early rabbinic period that four cups of wine should be consumed during the Passover meal; indeed, this law appears at the very beginning of the Mishnah on this topic: "They must not give them less than four cups of wine to drink" (*m. Pes.* 10:1). Yet later rabbis disputed whether there were in fact to be four or five cups of wine. In the Talmud, the question is left unresolved; for later Jews, however, a decision had to be made as to what the proper procedure was. Maimonides thus decided that though there should be five cups, only four were to be consumed. What, then, to do with that extraneous fifth cup? It was only in the fifteenth century that it was connected with the figure of Elijah. This link, however, was not entirely out of the blue:

Elijah had, since the earliest days of Judaism, been understood as the harbinger of the eschaton (a tradition picked up perhaps most famously in Christianity), and, as we have already seen in the Mishnah, the Passover Seder looked forward to the future redemption of Israel. With the assignment of the fifth cup to Elijah, that ancient aspect of the Seder ritual was brought to the forefront.

Almost every expansion of the Haggadah built on existing aspects of the ceremony, either practical or conceptual, ensuring that the deeper meanings of the ancient ritual acts would be apparent for all future generations. Perhaps the most recent development, however, is more a response to the changing nature of Judaism, at least in certain communities. In many Reform Jewish households, it has become customary to place an orange on the ceremonial Seder plate in the center of the table, along with the traditional elements. The orange is obviously out of place—and that is precisely the point. This new tradition was started in the 1980s by the Jewish feminist scholar Susanna Heschel, who suggested that it signaled support for gay Jews: as gay members of the community might feel marginalized, the orange symbolizes their equal place at the metaphorical table of Jewish life. Heschel's orange both participates in the traditional form of the Seder, by being part of the ancient Seder plate, and at the same time recognizes that as the Jewish community changes, ritual needs to change along with it. The orange is expansive, adding to the tradition, rather than restrictive or dismissive of the past. It is, in its way, no different from any of the other changes made to the Seder over the centuries. It reinforces a central part of the Seder: the claim that all Jews alive today—regardless of social standing—should see themselves as part of the Exodus story.

The Eucharist

Writing in the third century CE, the church father Origen proclaimed a direct link between the Exodus from Egypt and the death of Jesus: "We were saved at this time in Egypt, so we are saved at this time now."[5] The timing of Jesus's crucifixion, on the Jewish festival of Passover, was no coincidence. The salvation of Israel had happened again, for the new Israel of the Christian community. As the Exodus story was transformed by early Christians into a foreshadowing of the passion, so too the ritual expression of the Passover was reappropriated for its new meaning.

For the Synoptic Gospels—Matthew, Mark, and Luke—the identification of Jesus's Last Supper with the Passover Seder is uncontested and explicit (Matt 26:17–19; Mark 14:12–16; Luke 22:7–13). It is at this meal that Jesus proclaims what has become known as the Institution: "Take, eat; this is my body . . . Drink from it, all of you, for this is my blood of the covenant" (Matt 26:26–28). Some scholars have noted (not without challenges from others) that underlying these seminal statements is the regular Seder practice of holding up the matza and other elements of the Seder plate and defining their symbolic meanings.[6] "This is my body" stands in place of the Haggadah's "This is the bread of affliction." Jesus, in this way, is both participating in the traditional Passover Seder and simultaneously reinterpreting it. (This is even clearer in Luke's version, which mentions multiple cups of wine, both before and after the meal, as is required in a Seder.)

Notably, Jesus picks up on the central conceit of the Passover Seder: the ritual as a site of communal memory. "He took a loaf of bread, and when he had given thanks, he broke it and gave it to them, saying, 'This is my body, which is given for you. Do this in remembrance of me'" (Luke 22:19; see also 1 Cor 11:24–25). As Jesus celebrates the memory of Israel's past, he exhorts his followers to celebrate his own memory. The redemption from Egypt is replaced, or at least supplemented, with the redemption that Jesus brings. Memory remains ritualized as the ritual is imbued with new meaning.

Only implicit in the Synoptic Gospels is the identification of Jesus with the Passover sacrifice itself. Though both Mark and Luke take care to say that the Last Supper took place on the "day of Unleavened Bread, when the Passover lamb is sacrificed," they do not draw the direct connection between that Jewish ritual and the imminent sacrifice of Jesus. The Gospel of John, however, leaves no room for doubt: not only is Jesus referred to as "the Lamb of God" (John 1:29, 36), but the crucified body of Jesus is explicitly equated with that of the sacrificed Passover offering, with reference to an obscure law in Exodus 12:46: when the soldiers come to take down Jesus's body from the cross, "they did not break his legs . . . so that scripture might be fulfilled, 'None of his bones shall be broken'" (John 19:33, 36). Paul is similarly unequivocal: "Our paschal lamb, Christ, has been sacrificed" (1 Cor 5:7).

For the author of the Gospel of John, the direct identification of Jesus with the Passover sacrifice required making a small but significant adjustment to the narrative presented in the Synoptic Gospels. If, for the Synoptics, Jesus was celebrating Passover during the Last Supper—"on the day of Unleavened Bread, when the Passover lamb is sacrificed"— then Jesus's death would occur a day after the ritual slaughter of the lamb. John therefore moves the Last Supper a day earlier: "before the festival of Passover" (John 13:1). Now it is not the Last Supper that is aligned with the time of the Passover sacrifice but the crucifixion, as John makes clear: Pilate's decision to crucify Jesus is said to occur on "the day of Preparation for the Passover, and it was about noon" (John 19:14). This has the crucifixion occur not only on the right day but even at approximately the right time: in the afternoon, before the festival commences that evening with the consumption of the offering.

The lamb sacrificed in the book of Exodus has two functions: its blood is put on the doorposts and lintels of the Israelite homes in order to protect them, so that they can be rescued from Egypt; and its body is consumed by the Israelites during that night of vigil, a meal that becomes a formalized ritual of commemoration. So too—if not for John, then at least in a canonical reading of the New Testament—for the new lamb, Jesus: the blood that is shed at the crucifixion redeems his followers; his body is consumed symbolically at the Last Supper and onward as a ritualized site of memory.

For early Christians, the identification of Jesus with the paschal lamb, and thus of the death of Jesus with Passover, entailed a reinterpretation of the Exodus story itself. No longer was the redemption from Egypt the primary historical event to be commemorated or ritually revisited. Yet it could not be ignored: Jesus himself celebrated it, and as the statement from Origen at the beginning of this section shows, the symbolic power of Jesus's death is firmly rooted in the lasting power of the Exodus story. The early church father Irenaeus wrote, "He saved the children of Israel, showing forth in a mystery the passion of Christ by the immolation of a spotless lamb and its blood . . . and the name of this mystery is the Passover."[7] The Exodus remains, naturally, a historical event; it occurred not (only) for its own sake, however, but for the sake of looking forward to the death of Jesus. Origen similarly wrote, "This, then, is the way in which we would summarize the meaning of Christ sacrificed as our Pascha . . . the corporeal things are types of spiritual realities and the historical events represent ideal realities."[8] For Origen, this meant that while the Jews actually consume the flesh of the lamb "in a carnal way," Christians are to eat "the flesh of the Word of God. . . . Whoever can feed on them with perfect understanding and a purified heart, that man truly offers the sacrifice of the paschal festival."[9]

Origen seems to suggest that the redemptive function of Passover is now available at all times, to those who feast on the word of God. Nevertheless, early Christians maintained a regular ceremony by which they commemorated, among other things, Jesus's reinterpretation of the Passover Seder: the consumption of Jesus's body and blood in the ritual known as the Lord's Supper, or the Eucharist ("Thanksgiving"). What's more, they continued, at Easter, to observe something akin to Passover, or, as they called it in Aramaic (and Greek), Pascha.[10]

In the first centuries of Christianity, there was a dispute as to when Pascha should be celebrated. Some maintained the date established in the Jewish calendar, the fourteenth of Nisan, for which they were termed Quartodecimans. This view, most prominently preserved in the *Peri Pascha* of Melito of Sardis, a second-century bishop in modern-day Turkey, was eventually deemed heretical at the Council of Nicaea in the early fourth century. Most Christians observed Pascha on the Sunday following Passover, both because that was the day of Jesus's resurrection and because

Sunday had already been established as the weekly Christian Sabbath. What had once been the Passover Seder—an evening affair that could last into the next morning, as the midrash of the rabbis in the Haggadah describes—was replaced by a fast and vigil the Saturday night before Easter Sunday. The Christian vigil retained the narrative elements of the Seder, telling the stories of both the Exodus and of Jesus's death and resurrection, but the element of the meal was delayed until the Eucharist the next morning.

The Eucharist itself was not tied exclusively to Easter Sunday. The ritual consumption of Christ's body and blood took place at regular communal gatherings called "agape" by early Christians, at which the community of Jesus's followers was reinforced. Those meals became less frequent, giving way to Christian prayer services that included the reading of biblical passages, and thus the Eucharist gradually moved from the table to the altar, from a meal to a more distinctive form of worship. (In this way, Christianity unwittingly reversed the very shift from altar to table that the rabbis had instituted with the creation of the Seder in the first place.) The Eucharist also began to be surrounded by regular prayers, along with the reading of those biblical passages that explained its meaning, that is, the Institution: "This is my body."

The church father Eusebius made clear that the Eucharist was both the Christian replacement for Passover and was to be severed from the annual Jewish festival. "Moses's followers used to sacrifice the paschal sheep only once a year, on the fourteenth of the first month, toward evening; but we of the New Testament, performing our Pascha every Lord's day, are always satiating ourselves with the saving body and always partaking of the sheep's blood." Life in

Christ was a constant experience of the Exodus: "We are always departing from Egypt; we are always seeking after the lonely desert of human life; we are always setting out on the journey towards God; we are always celebrating the Crossing-Feast [i.e., Passover]." And as this is not an annual experience, but an ever-present one, its celebration should perhaps not even be confined just to Sundays: "For the gospel word would have us do these things not once a year but always, even daily. And that is why we keep the feast of our Pascha every week on the salvific Day of the Lord."[11]

Eusebius points to a conscious and persistent anti-Judaism trend in the development of the Eucharist, one that is most evident in the rejection of the calendrical timing of the Jewish festival—including the decision to deem the Quartodeciman practice heretical: the emperor Constantine's letter to the Council of Nicaea declared it "unsuitable that we should celebrate that holy festival following the custom of the Jews"—but also entailed a repudiation of the literal fleshly consumption of the Passover offering. This latter point is somewhat ironic. In the first place, the rabbinic Passover Seder had already rendered the paschal offering nonliteral, replacing it with matza and giving it symbolic meaning. Second, some Christian communities reliteralized the Eucharist, declaring that the consumption of the bread and wine at the Lord's Supper was in fact the literal consumption of Jesus's body and blood.

Despite attempts to de-Judaize, two of the most basic conceptual aspects of the Jewish Passover Seder were retained in the ritual of the Eucharist. The first, already noted with regard to Jesus's own words at the Last Supper, is the Eucharist as a site of memory. Just as the Passover Seder serves as a guarantee that the memory of God's redemption of Israel should not be lost among Jews, so too the Eucharist is a regular reminder of the sacrifice that Jesus made for Christians. In both, that memory is reinforced in both a ritual act of eating and in the retelling of the story, complete with biblical passages to be recited and interpreted. Both entail a specificity of reference, historically and symbolically.

Additionally, both the Jewish Seder and the Christian Eucharist employ an explicit rhetoric of continuity between past and present. In the Seder, this comes out in the Haggadah: "In every generation a man must so regard himself as if he came forth himself out of Egypt." Through the Passover ritual every Jew, in every time and place, becomes a participant in the ongoing redemption of Israel. In the Eucharist, the weekly (or even daily) act of consuming the bread and wine implicates the worshipper in the eternal salvation of Jesus. The story of Jesus's death—like that of the paschal lamb in Exodus—is lifted from its historical context and made available for the present, in all presents. As Martin Luther wrote, Christians should "remember our exodus from Egypt, and in remembrance of it return to Him who brought us out through the washing of the new birth. Now this we can do most advantageously of all in the sacrament of the bread and wine."[12] Both Jews and Christians are called to personally appropriate the narrative, and, through ritual, to collapse time and space.

Conclusion

Just as the Passover Seder evolved over time, so too, of course, did the ritual of the Eucharist. Various Christian denominations celebrate the Eucharist at different times—daily, weekly, more sporadically. The prayers that accompany the ritual differ from community to community. The question of what should constitute the bread is hardly consistent: for some it is actual bread, for others, such as Catholics, it is the communion wafer, meant to represent the unleavened bread of the Exodus. (These matters can get quite arcane—recently the Catholic Church reiterated that the wafer must contain at least a trace amount of gluten.)

The Easter Vigil, which had once been the central Christian representation of the Passover, gradually lost importance, as the focus of Easter moved consistently away from Jesus's death and toward the resurrection, and as Good Friday emerged as a fundamental part, first of the triduum, the three days leading up to Easter, and then of the more expansive Holy Week. In recent years, however, as communities have been rediscovering traditional forms of worship, the Easter Vigil has undergone a revival in some traditions. In addition, some Christians have begun to celebrate an authentic Passover Seder, either on the Thursday of Holy Week (in line with the Johannine narrative) or on Passover itself. This is often done as a way of walking in Jesus's footsteps, as it were, a form of *imitatio Christi*. But it also serves as a reminder that the power of the ritual has remained consistent even over two thousand years of history, theological changes, and fraught Jewish-Christian relations. Whether in the Seder or in the Eucharist, the Exodus story still stands as a central point in Judeo-Christian self-understanding.

FIG. 4: Rembrandt, *Moses Breaking the Tablets of the Law* (1659).

Sinai and the Law

While the ritualizations of Exodus focus on the moment of redemption, the Exodus story does not end with the Passover. Indeed, in the biblical narrative, the departure from Egypt is not an ending but a beginning, even a preliminary step, toward the central moment of the Pentateuch as a whole: the theophany and law-giving at the mountain in the wilderness. (Though the mountain is identified by two different names in the Pentateuch—Sinai and Horeb—this is commonly known as the Sinai event, and for the sake of ease we will use "Sinai" to represent the canonical narrative.)

Textually, the Sinai event covers by far the most material in the Pentateuch, and indeed more than any other event in the entire Bible: from Exodus 19 all the way through Numbers 10, a total of fifty-eight chapters. Conceptually, it is even broader: this is the moment toward which the entire narrative builds—certainly that of Exodus, and in many ways that of Genesis as well. The Sinai event, at least in the Hebrew Bible, is the answer to the question "Why?": Why did God free the Israelites, why did he choose Abraham and his descendants, why, even, did he create humanity in the first place?

For later traditions of both Judaism and Christianity, the centrality of the Sinai event did not diminish, though it was differently recognized and interpreted. At stake, underlying these various readings, was the issue of the law: a binding system for Judaism, an obsolete one for Christianity. Both approaches, however, were bound by the incontrovertible importance of Sinai, historically and symbolically. This was, after all, the moment when Israel's God revealed himself to the people as a whole, standing at the foot of the mountain; when Israel heard God's words directly, and, crucially, when the covenant between God and the people of Israel was firmly cemented. Any understanding of the relationship between Israel—whether the old Israel or the new one of Christianity—and its deity could hardly avoid being grounded in this seminal event.

In many ways, the different perspectives that Judaism and Christianity brought to bear on the Sinai event were foundational for erecting a conceptual barrier between the two developing religions. The status of the law and the nature of the divine revelation, central to the Exodus story, are central also to the very identities of Judaism and Christianity from their early years down to the present.

Sinai and the Law in the Hebrew Bible

The redemption of the Israelites from Egypt was predicated on the promise that God had made with the patriarchs Abraham, Isaac, and Jacob—that their ancestors would come to possess the land of Canaan: "I established my covenant with them, to give them the land of Canaan . . . I have heard the groaning of the Israelites whom the Egyptians are holding as slaves, and I have remembered my covenant"

(Exod 6:4, 5). But God's previous covenant with the limited group of Abraham and his descendants was in need of updating, in recognition of the newly defined nation of Israel. Thus God went on: "I will take you as my people, and I will be your God" (6:7). This relationship would require a new covenant, with new terms: no longer a unilateral promise but a bilateral agreement, complete with stipulations and commitments on both sides. This is the covenant made at Sinai.

The first words that Israel hears from God in the divine speech that includes the Ten Commandments are a striking and important self-definition: "I am Yahweh your God, who brought you out of the land of Egypt" (Exod 20:2). No longer is God defined as the deity of the ancestors; for Israel, God's identity is inextricable from the historical redemption that has just taken place. The Exodus may have been grounded in the patriarchal promises, but it would now be put to use as the grounds for a new arrangement, one based on the laws that would follow. "You have seen what I did to the Egyptians, and how I bore you on eagles' wings and brought you to myself. Now, therefore, if you obey my voice and keep my covenant, you shall be my treasured possession out of all the peoples" (Exod 19:3–4).

Even before they have heard the laws, the stipulations of this covenant, the Israelites accede to God's terms: "Everything that Yahweh has spoken, we will do" (19:8). After the giving of the Ten Commandments and the three chapters of law that follow in Exodus 21–23, known as the Covenant Code, the people reaffirm their commitment, in the same language (24:3). And they do so for a third time after a formal covenant ceremony, which includes Moses's rereading of the laws to the community: "All that Yahweh has spoken we will do, and we will be obedient" (24:7).

At the conclusion of Leviticus, the set of cultic regulations delivered by God to Moses from the tabernacle at the foot of Sinai, the true nature of the Exodus is plainly stated. Though God had freed the Israelites from Egypt, in doing so he merely shifted their obligation from a human king to the divine ruler. "To me the people of Israel are slaves; they are my slaves, whom I brought out from the land of Egypt: I am Yahweh your God" (Lev 25:55). Though this may be some of the strongest such language in the Bible, it is representative of the basic notion found throughout the Pentateuch. The Exodus, more than freeing the Israelites, imposed upon them an obligation to the God who had redeemed them. That obligation is expressed in law: in the civil laws of the Covenant Code, in the cultic laws of Leviticus, and in the comprehensive almost-constitution of Deuteronomy. (Though the laws of Deuteronomy are delivered to the Israelites by Moses on the last day of his life in the plains of Moab just across the Jordan from Canaan, they had been given to Moses back at the mountain in the wilderness, and they are both introduced and regularly punctuated by reminders of the obligation the Exodus entailed. In words that were picked up by the Haggadah: "When your children ask you in time to come, 'What is the meaning of the decrees and the statutes and the ordinances that Yahweh our God has commanded you?' then you shall say to your children, 'We were Pharaoh's slaves in Egypt, but Yahweh brought us out of Egypt with a mighty hand'" [Deut 6:20–21].)

At the end of the laws in Leviticus, and again at the end of the laws in Deuteronomy, faithful obedience is framed as a choice between curse and blessing. Obedience will bring divine protection, agricultural production, and prosperity in the promised land; disobedience will result in divine abandonment, agricultural failure, external attack, and exile. The laws, as scholars have long noted, are presented as the stipulations of a treaty, in line with standard ancient Near Eastern practice. The blessing and curses are a traditional part of this generic form—and so too is the historical preface, in which the dominant party lays out the reasons why the subordinate party is obligated to accept the terms. That historical preface for the laws of the Pentateuch is the Exodus.

Structurally, then, the Exodus proper is merely the prelude to the laws. This is not to diminish its importance—it is absolutely necessary and stands as the high-water mark in God's actions in history on behalf of Israel—but neither should it overshadow the laws that follow it: it was for the sake of the laws that the story was written.

Sinai and Law in Judaism

The centrality of the laws in the Pentateuch was not in question for the classical rabbis of the early first millennium. Huge amounts of text, including the Mishnah, the Talmud, and the various corpora of legal midrash, were dedicated to understanding, coordinating, and applying the biblical laws. The rabbis were equally conscious of the relative status of the laws over against the narrative, inquiring, "Why does the Torah not begin in Exodus 12?," that is, with the laws of the Passover offering. (An alternative version of this rabbinic question asks why the Torah does not begin with the Ten Commandments.) Their answer is very much in line with what we have already seen from the Bible itself. The narratives, including all of Genesis, provide the explanation for who the Israelites are and why they are required to obey the divine commands. "The Omnipresent brought out the Israelites from Egypt, divided the sea for them, raised up for them the well, brought them a flight of quails, and waged for them the war with Amalek. Then he said to them, 'Let me reign over you.' They responded, 'Yes, yes'" (*Mek.* Bahodesh 5). As the great scholar of rabbinic traditions Ephraim Urbach put it, "All that preceded—the history of the patriarchs, the bondage of Egypt, and the Exodus—is not of primary importance. All these are to be understood as preparatory events."[1] Even in the Haggadah, the ritual telling of the Exodus story, the song "Dayyenu" celebrates not only the redemption from Egypt but also the giving of the law.

As we saw in chapter 2, some early Jewish authors living in the midst of the dominant Greco-Roman culture took great pains to articulate a cogent defense of Jewish law in terms that would be familiar to their non-Jewish neighbors. Thus Philo, for example, equated the biblical legislation with the philosophical concept of natural law, appealing to Stoic ideas of rationality and immutability: "Whoever will carefully examine the nature of the particular enactments will find that they seek to attain to the harmony of the universe and are in agreement with the principles of eternal nature" (*Mos.* 2.52). By broadening the notion of the law to encompass not only its Jewish adherents but the entire universe, Philo effectively removed the laws from the historical, biblical context. Indeed, many of the Jewish writers of this period, as they grappled with prevalent Greco-Roman traditions, shifted their focus away from the historically contingent laws given by Moses and toward a more expansive notion of law as representative of wisdom, or *sophia*.

Later generations of Jewish writers and thinkers, the classical rabbis of the first millennium CE, turned against this trend toward equating biblical law with natural law. While Philo tried to understand the laws of Moses as participating in comprehensible and rational categories, the rabbis explicitly affirmed the irrationality—or at least the incomprehensibility—of the biblical legislation.[2] They famously pointed to the laws regarding the wearing of ritual fringes in Numbers 15: "Speak to the Israelite people and instruct them to make for themselves fringes on the corners of their garments throughout the ages; let them attach a cord of blue to the fringe at each corner" (15:38). This is perhaps the paradigmatic irrational law—there is no natural explanation for why people should wear a certain decorative item on their clothing—and the rabbis were fully aware of the issue. It was not, however, a problem for them, in part precisely because the law is followed by a reference to the Exodus story: "I am Yahweh your God, who brought you out of the land of Egypt to be your God: I, Yahweh, am your God" (15:41).

The rabbis asked:

Why mention the exodus from Egypt in connection with the detailing of each commandment? ... When the Holy One, blessed be he, redeemed the seed of Abraham his friend, he did not redeem them as free men, but as slaves. If he should make a decree and they do not accept it, he will say to them, "You are my slaves." When they went out into the desert, he began to issue decrees for them—some light commandments and some heavier commandments, such as the Sabbath and the sexual prohibitions, fringes and tefillin. Israel began to object. He said to them, "You are my slaves. For this reason I redeemed you: so that I can make decrees for you and you will fulfill them." (*Sifre Bem. Shelah* 115)

The mention of the Exodus in the context of the laws is not a mere reminder of Israel's redemption; it is a means of coercion. Following the biblical reference to Israel as God's slaves cited above, the rabbis understand that the laws are not a matter of choice or even of reason. Israel is obligated to obey the laws because of the Exodus, not because the laws are sensible or desirable. Indeed, the laws are often acknowledged as undesirable—this is true particularly of the laws of sexual morality in Leviticus 18 and 20—and yet the Israelites are required to adhere to them nonetheless. Again, we see that the Exodus serves as the answer to the question "Why?": Why on earth should Jews wear ritual fringes? Because of the Exodus—and there is no more that should be or can be explained. "The acknowledgment of the exodus from Egypt means the acceptance of the yoke of the kingdom of Heaven; the denial of the Exodus signifies the refusal to accept that yoke."[3]

The perspective that the contents of the laws are, or at least can be, fundamentally irrational, and are to be obeyed merely because God imposed them on Israel, is not quite as nihilistic as it first appears. For the rabbis, the very fact that the laws have no intrinsic human motivation, or in some cases run counter to natural human desires, means that obedience is more valuable. As Christine Hayes correctly puts it, "Virtue attaches to and arises from the performance of commandments, *particularly* the commandments that are difficult to accept because they are illogical, arbitrary, and counter to one's natural desires."[4] In this sense, the biblical laws are worth following precisely because they are distinct from natural law.

Other rabbinic texts affirm the value of the incomprehensibility of the laws differently. Obeying laws that otherwise make little logical sense necessarily honors the power that authored and enforces those laws, that is, God. And again, it is especially those laws that defy explanation that more clearly enhance the status of the deity. Hayes again, describing this rabbinic position: "The *only* rationale for obeying the law is to affirm the sovereignty of its author, in which case the substance of the law is entirely immaterial."[5]

In a sense, the irrationality of the divine laws—along with the inconsistencies that are present across the law codes of Exodus, Leviticus, and Deuteronomy, as a result of their distinct authorships—permitted the rise of the entire rabbinic system of legal discourse. Granted that the laws were to be obeyed despite their essential incomprehensibility, the practical questions of how the laws were to be enacted became the focus of rabbinic exegesis. The endless disputes and discussions about the laws—what was known as the Oral Torah—were understood by the rabbis not as human attempts to understand the inexplicable but as a part of the divine plan from the beginning.

This is illustrated in the first place by the famous opening of the mishnaic tractate Pirkei Avot: "Moses received the Law from Sinai and committed it to Joshua, and Joshua to the elders, and the elders to the prophets, and the prophets committed it to the men of the Great Synagogue" (*m. Avot* 1:1). "The Law" here is the Oral Torah; that is, the interpretation of the Torah is understood to have been given along with the written Torah all the way back at Sinai. As the famous Rabbi Akiva put it, "The Torah, with its laws and details and interpretations, was given by Moses at Sinai" (*Sifra* Be-Huqqotay 8:2). Even the rabbinic disputes of the first millennium CE thus have their roots in the Exodus story: the Exodus is the rationale for rabbinic law just as much as it is for biblical law.

Moreover, the rabbis held that once the law had been given at Sinai, it was now in human hands. This meant that its ostensible meaning could be adjusted for new situations, and its wording could be mined for senses that are nowhere apparent in the biblical text. The famous rabbinic expression of this is the phrase "The Torah is not in heaven." Amazingly, this claim is invoked when, in the midst of a legal dispute, a heavenly voice sides with one party over another.[6] That heavenly voice is rejected as a source of legal authority. For the rabbis, this is not to contravene biblical law but rather to more fully live into it. The obligation of the Sinai event is a permanent one, but its application is variable, or at least always up for discussion. By not only permitting the ongoing interpretation of the law but in fact requiring it as a part of the obligation imposed by the Exodus and invoked by God at Sinai, the rabbis created a system that ensured the continuing vitality of Judaism, even after the destruction of the temple and the resulting lapse into desuetude of so much cult-centered biblical law.

In many modern Jewish communities, the law—whether biblical or rabbinic—is no longer followed, or at least not with anything near the comprehensiveness of more traditional communities past and present. And yet the rabbinic innovations regarding the law continue to be relevant. It is, of course, the irrationality of the laws, or at least the increasing difficulty of following them in modern society, that is in large part responsible for the decreasing adherence to them. But the underlying sense of obligation remains, even if only in an attenuated and perhaps implicit form. That obligation is often fulfilled not by obedience to the laws but by the study of the biblical and rabbinic texts. Indeed, the classical rabbis had already anticipated this to a degree: "If you have studied much in the Law, much reward will be given you" (*m. Avot* 2:16). The laws themselves are crucial, of course, but "the study of Torah is equal to them all" (*m. Peah* 1:1). The rabbis certainly did not intend that study of the laws should replace fulfillment of the laws—rather, they say quite explicitly that study without obedience is for naught—but they did provide a mechanism, two thousand years ago, for modern Jews to feel a connection with the legal traditions of the past even in the absence of total compliance.

The Status of the Law in Early Christianity

While rabbinic Judaism took up the position of the Hebrew Bible, seeing the laws as an obligation imposed on

Israel by God, to be followed despite, or even precisely because of, their essential irrationality, Christianity developed a very different view of the law, and of the nature of the Sinai event. There are hints in the New Testament of an early adherence to the laws of the Pentateuch, most notably in the Gospel of Matthew, in which Jesus says, "Do not think that I have come to abolish the law or the prophets . . . For truly I tell you, until heaven and earth pass away, not one letter, not one stroke of a letter, will pass from the law until all is accomplished" (Matt 5:17–18). But the predominant opinion for the history of Christian thought is that of Paul. And while Paul is himself not entirely consistent on this issue, he introduced a critique of the law that has lasted down to the present.[7]

Paul distinguished between Jews and Gentiles, allowing the former to continue observing the law but rejecting it for the latter. In part, this seeming inconsistency may be chalked up to Paul's rhetorical aims. If what he wants is to bring everyone, both Jew and Gentile, into the community of Jesus followers, then allowing each group to maintain its present cultural norms, neither giving up a long legal heritage nor adopting foreign customs, was simply a practical decision. Insofar as the vast majority of those who did accept the Christian faith were not Jews but Gentiles, the anti-law position became the de facto standard for Christianity from the beginning. The rejection of the law (and with it, intentionally or not, a strong anti-Jewish sentiment) stands as a significant part of Paul's legacy.

In his appeals to Gentile audiences, Paul directly strikes at many of the same issues that we have already seen in biblical and early Jewish discourses about the law. Like the rabbis, he rejects Philo's attempts to equate biblical law with natural law. "If it had not been for the law, I would not have known sin. I would not have known what it is to covet if the law had not said, 'You shall not covet'" (Rom 7:7–8). Though perhaps a strange example—covetousness seeming to be a fairly consistent element of human desire—Paul's argument here is plain. The laws are not in line with nature. Indeed, the laws introduce new concepts and categories of sin that have no equivalent in the natural order. Totally normal behavior—wearing clothing without ritual fringes, for instance—is sinful under the law. That this sort of sin should be punishable by death is, for Paul, to say that the law leads to death: "I was once alive apart from the law, but when the commandment came, sin revived and I died and the very commandment that promised life proved to be death to me" (Rom 7:8–10).

Paul agrees with the rabbis in that the biblical laws are a coercive imposition, even to the point of using the metaphor of slavery. "Now we are discharged from the law, dead to that which held us captive, so that we are slaves not under the old written code but in the new life of the Spirit" (Rom 7:6). In Leviticus, God claims that the Israelites are slaves to him; Paul reads this as the Israelites being enslaved not to the truth of God, that is, the Spirit, but to the letter of the law. There is a proper sort of slavery for Paul, therefore—but it is not to the law, which is a sort of slavery to death.

The major step for Paul comes in his view that the law was not, as the rabbis understood it, the ultimate goal of the divine plan for Israel. Paul reverses the traditional Jewish hierarchy of law and narrative, setting the narrative—specifically, the promises to the patriarchs—above the revelation of the law at Sinai. In the promise to Abraham, Paul finds the authentic divine message. Again, this choice may in part stem from the relative universality of the patriarchal promise—at the very least, God tells Abraham that "all the families of the earth" will be affected by Abraham's being blessed—as compared to the quite strict particularity of the laws given at Sinai. James Dunn cogently writes, "What Paul was endeavoring to do was to free both promise and law for a wider range of recipients, freed from the ethnic constraints which he saw to be narrowing the grace of God and diverting the saving purpose of God out of its main channel—Christ."[8] As the more universal and less "ethnically constrained" aspect of the divine-human relationship, the patriarchal promises were more easily adopted for Gentile audiences, in no small part also because they entail no specific behavior. All they require is faith, as Paul famously says: "Just as 'Abraham believed God, and it was reckoned to him as righteousness' [Gen 15:6], so, you see, those who believe are the descendants of Abraham" (Gal 3:6–7). (Paul, by focusing on Abraham, does force himself to confront the question of circumcision elsewhere. He does so by appealing to the fact that Abraham's righteousness was conferred on him in Genesis 15, before the requirement of circumcision two chapters later.)

The promise to Abraham, in Paul's view, does not speak solely to the expansion of a family into a nation and the possession of Canaan but looks ahead to the arrival and salvation of Jesus. If Jesus is the fulfillment of the promise, however, where does that leave the laws of Sinai? For Paul, they were always subordinate, and, crucially, temporary: "The law, which came four hundred thirty years later, does not annul a covenant previously ratified by God, so as to nullify the promise" (Gal 3:17). Rather than being eternal, as was the promise to Abraham, the laws of Sinai were intended by God to keep Israel in a state of constant awareness of sin— until Jesus came to relieve them of it. "Before faith came, we were imprisoned and guarded under the law until faith would be revealed. Therefore the law was our disciplinarian until Christ came, so that we might be justified by faith. But now that faith has come, we are no longer subject to a disciplinarian" (Gal 3:23–25).

In order for Paul to make this argument, he must reckon with the fact that he is prioritizing one divine covenant, the patriarchal promise, over another divine covenant, the one made at Sinai. Here he can rely on the theme of the new covenant that we have already explored in chapter 2. It is precisely the covenant at Sinai, made in Exodus 24 on the basis of the laws found in the preceding chapters, that Jesus alludes to at the Last Supper. Paul renarrates that event in 1 Corinthians 11, and refers to the new covenant elsewhere, including 2 Corinthians 3:6, where he claims that God "has made us competent to be ministers of a new covenant, not of the letter but of the Spirit; for the letter kills, but the Spirit gives life." Again, it is apparent that for Paul this new covenant is not simply an addition to those given to Israel in the past but is quite specifically a replacement for the covenant at Sinai, that is, for the laws. As Paul says in Romans 10:4: "Christ is the end of the law"— though the Greek word for "end" here, *telos*, can also have the meaning of "goal" or "aim"; Paul may have had both meanings in mind.

Through these rhetorical moves, Paul not only severs the link that Philo attempted to draw between biblical law and natural law, but he puts the two in direct competition. He understands the laws of Sinai as specific to both a people and a time, both of which have now been superseded by the coming of Jesus. The new covenant returns to the original covenant, the promise to Abraham, made before the advent of the laws, with its universalistic framework. Given this stark dichotomy, it is no surprise that Christian writers following Paul took up and even more vigorously argued his rejection of the law.

The earliest of these may have been the author of the letter to the Hebrews, who wrote in Paul's name but is recognized by modern scholars as pseudepigraphic. "If that first covenant had been faultless, there would have been no need to look for a second one," we read in Hebrews 8:7. A few verses later: "In speaking of 'a new covenant,' he has made the first one obsolete. And what is obsolete and growing old will soon disappear" (8:13). The author of Hebrews even refers to the new covenant as "eternal" (13:20), thereby more firmly identifying the earlier covenant, that of Sinai, as temporary. These are Paul's ideas, but expressed with somewhat more vitriol toward Judaism.

The writings of the early church are replete with antagonism toward the law, and toward the Jews who kept it. Justin Martyr, in his dialogue with the Jew Trypho, writes, "Law placed against law has abrogated that which is before it, and a covenant which comes after in like manner has put an end the previous one; and an eternal and final law—namely, Christ—has been given to us, and the covenant is trustworthy, after which there shall be no law, no commandment, no ordinance" (*Trypho* 11). Justin goes on to accuse Trypho, and the Jews generally, of despising and slighting the new covenant, and therefore of willfully disobeying God—a rhetorical twist that goes well beyond Paul's fairly commodious attitude toward Jewish observance.

Tertullian, the second- to third-century church father, furthered Paul's dissociation of Jewish law with natural law, arguing that there was divine law before Moses. Moreover, this divine law was for all: "Why should God, the founder of the universe, the governor of the whole world, the fashioner of humanity, the sower of universal nations, be believed to have given a law through Moses to one people, and not be said to have assigned it to all nations?" (*Answer to the Jews*, chapter 2). This effectively denies the status of divine law to the Pentateuch; at the very least, Tertullian says, "it should be believed to have been temporarily observed and kept." The advent of Jesus, of course, marks clearly the end of that temporary period: "There is incumbent on us a necessity . . . to show and prove, on the one hand, that the old Law has ceased, and on the other, that the promised new law is now in operation" (*Answer to the Jews*, chapter 6). (This proof, of course, is drawn from the words of the Hebrew Bible itself, from the prophets most significantly, which are read as inescapably pointing to Jesus. In the third century, Cyprian wrote an entire three-volume work entitled "Testimonies against the Jews," consisting of little other than headings—"That the former law which was given by Moses was to cease," for example—followed by proof texts from the Hebrew Bible.)

Another common tactic was to acknowledge the law as valid but to reconfigure it. Some claimed that Jesus was the fulfillment not only of the promise to Abraham but of the laws of Moses. Others argued that the law was meant to be interpreted spiritually rather than literally. In the latter camp we find Augustine, who wrote with reference to a verse from the prophet Malachi: "He intends also that they learn to interpret the law spiritually, and find Christ in it" (*City of God*, chapter 28). Augustine castigates those who read the law "carnally without perceiving that its earthly promises were figures of things spiritual."

In furthering Paul's rhetoric of the law as a form of slavery, some early Christian writers denigrated Jews as people who were willingly choosing to be enslaved. Augustine says that the grace of Christ "condemns not that Law, but invites us at length to yield obedience to its love, not to be slaves to the fear of the Law. Itself is grace, that is, free gift, which they understand not to have come to them from God, who still desire to be under the bonds of the Law" (*On the Profit of Believing*, section 9). This move preserves the law as divine and worthy, but condemns those who continue to adhere to it.

Not only did the advent of Jesus alter the nature of biblical law in all of these ways, but for some authors Jesus was in fact a new law unto himself, either in his person or in the practice of the Christian faith. The Epistle of Barnabas claims that the old laws have been "abolished" in favor of "the new law of our Lord Jesus Christ" (Epistle of Barnabas, chapter 2). Tertullian refers to the gospel as "the law which is properly ours" (*On Monogamy*, chapter 8). In the early text known as the Shepherd of Hermas, we find reference to "the law of God that was given to the whole world, and this law is the Son of God" (Shepherd of Hermas, 3.8). As noted above, Justin Martyr describes Christ as "an eternal and final law." It is not law itself that is objectionable: it is the specific laws of Moses that are rejected, in favor of the law that is Jesus, or the gospel—the properly "natural" law.

Examples could easily be multiplied to fill this entire book and many others. The point, however, should be clear: though Paul was more ambivalent about the status of the biblical law than he is often given credit for, the trend in early Christianity, and in some cases down to the present, was to view the laws given at Sinai as having been superseded, at best, and as the source of sin and death for the Jews, at worst.

The Ten Commandments

Despite the rejection of the laws, however, early Christian authors did not go so far as to deny the importance of the Sinai event altogether. This would be to commit the heresy of Marcion, the denial of the Hebrew Bible in toto, a heresy against which numerous church fathers strongly argued. But while Sinai was equated with Mosaic law in Jewish tradition, it could not be so for Christianity, not if Sinai were to still maintain some semblance of relevance. It could also hardly be denied that the primary, if not sole, purpose of the Sinai event was the giving of divine commandments to Israel. Where Christian authors found redeeming value in the Sinai event was not in the vast and often arcane collections of laws delivered by Moses to the people but rather in the simple, elegant, and far more comprehensible laws spoken directly by God to Israel: the Ten Commandments, or the Decalogue. (The nomenclature is a matter of minor interest: the Hebrew of the Bible calls them "the ten words," which is equivalent to the Greek *dekalogos*, or Decalogue; it was the Geneva Bible and then the King James Bible that invented and popularized the name "Ten Commandments.")

The prominence of the Ten Commandments as a marker of Christianity is obvious today, most notably in the ongoing debates regarding whether monuments devoted to them can or should be set in front of courthouses and city halls across America. Given the traditional Christian antipathy toward Moses—or at least the laws that Moses came to represent—it is perhaps surprising that the most visually identifiable symbol of Moses, the tablets of the Decalogue, should be claimed so widely and publicly by Christians. Yet when viewed through the lens of early Christian thought, the appropriation of the Ten Commandments makes considerably more sense.

Already in the New Testament, the importance of the Decalogue is unmistakable. In the Synoptic Gospels, Jesus cites the second half of the Ten Commandments when asked how one may merit eternal life: "You know the commandments," he replies: "Do not murder, do not commit adultery, do not steal, do not bear false witness, honor your father and your mother" (Mark 10:19; Luke 18:20). In the letter to the Romans, Paul cites the same set of commandments as examples of how one person may love another, "for he who loves his neighbor has fulfilled the law" (Rom 13:8). As Paul makes clear, the working definition of "love your neighbor as yourself"—the golden rule, as it is often called—is obedience to the laws of the Decalogue.

For early Christian writers, the Decalogue was the epitome of natural law, in contradistinction to the unnatural laws that constituted the covenant at Sinai, especially the cultic regulations. Irenaeus, one of the earliest church fathers, writing in the late second century, claims that even the patriarchs, living before any law was given to Israel, "had the meaning of the Decalogue written in their hearts and souls" (*Against Heresies* 4.16). The "righteousness and love of God" that came naturally to Israel's ancestors, however, evaporated during the four hundred years of enslavement in Egypt, and so God proclaimed them again at Sinai. As the scholar Robert Grant put it, "The way in which the early church was able to systematize use of the Decalogue and provide a theological basis for its retention by gentiles was by extensive use of the idea that the law of nature and the law of God were essentially the same."[9]

The most salient aspect of the Decalogue was its direct delivery from God to the people, without Moses acting as intermediary. While the Mosaic laws were temporary, God's own speech is eternal and eternally binding: "The Lord himself did speak in his own person to all alike the words of the Decalogue; and therefore, in like manner, do they remain permanently with us," as Irenaeus put it (*Against Heresies* 4.16). Jesus rendered the Mosaic laws inoperative, but not so the Decalogue, which received "by means of his advent in the flesh extension and increase, but not abrogation." Thus the Decalogue is not only still in effect, it remains an absolute requirement: "which," Irenaeus writes, "if any one does not observe, he has no salvation" (*Against Heresies* 4.15).

Augustine, however, complicates the picture by pointing out, quite rightly, that when Paul writes in Romans that the law brings sin and death, the example he uses—"you shall not covet"—is actually from the Decalogue itself. Additionally, Paul refers to the "ministry of death, chiseled in letters on stone tablets" (2 Cor 3:7)—which sounds awfully like a reference to the Decalogue, inscribed on two stone tablets by the very finger of God. Augustine's solution to this dilemma is not to deny the lasting importance of the Decalogue, but he argues instead that what Paul means is that even the laws of the Decalogue are insufficient when not accompanied by the spiritual acceptance of Jesus. "The oldness of the letter, in the absence of the newness of the spirit" (*Treatise on the Spirit and the Letter*, chapter 26) is the problem. Even the one small segment of the law that Jews and Christians might mutually hold to is therefore taken away as a point of agreement: Jews can't be credited even with following the Ten Commandments if they do not also have faith in Jesus.

Ironically, even the Ten Commandments were not entirely acceptable for early Christians, despite being associated with natural law. There is the sticky matter of the Sabbath, which for Christians fell under the same heading as circumcision and other ritual matters such as the dietary laws, namely, an aspect of Jewish practice that was quite consciously abandoned. Thus Augustine, engaging in a sort of special pleading, says that "in the Decalogue, which was given on Mount Sinai, only the portion which relates to the Sabbath was hidden under a prefiguring precept" (*Treatise on the Spirit and the Letter*, chapter 27)—that is, points to something in the future (the revelation of Jesus), rather than simply meaning what it says. Elsewhere Augustine argues that Christians are still meant to follow the precepts of the Decalogue, "apart from the carnal observance of the Sabbath, which signifies spiritual sanctification and rest" (*Treatise against Two Letters of the Pelagians*, 3.10). Eventually, of course, Sabbath observance shifted to Sunday and, without the detailed legal observances of Judaism, would become part of Christian life, beginning in the reign of Constantine in the fourth century.

In part as a result of the Christian fixation on the Ten Commandments as the only truly binding law of the Hebrew Bible, it is commonly assumed that they have always been as significant as we now consider them to be. But within the context of the Hebrew Bible itself, this is not entirely true. The Ten Commandments appear twice in the Pentateuch: in Exodus 20 and in Deuteronomy 5 (the latter being Moses's recollection of their original proclamation in the wilderness). That they appear twice is not necessarily an indication of their importance: after all, Deuteronomy contains the rehearsal of numerous episodes that were narrated originally in Exodus and Numbers. The Decalogue is, in that sense, no different from the stories of the spies, or the golden calf, or many others less well known. In fact, if repetition is to be taken as a marker of centrality, then the Ten Commandments are relatively less important than, say, the thrice-repeated law forbidding the Israelites to boil a kid in its mother's milk. When we look more globally at the Hebrew Bible as a whole, it is perhaps surprising that the Decalogue goes largely unmentioned outside of these two chapters in the Pentateuch. (Though some have sought to identify the occasional pseudo-Decalogue in other chapters and books of the Hebrew Bible, none of these arguments is particularly convincing—certainly none is as clear as the citations in the New Testament.)

Perhaps the first thorough treatment of the Ten Commandments as an independent legal unit came, unsurprisingly, from Philo, in his treatise "On the Decalogue." Philo, as noted in chapter 2, attempted to organize the bulk of the Mosaic laws under the headings provided by the Ten Commandments. This was part of his overall effort, as described above, to equate Jewish law with natural law. Since the Decalogue was, as early Christian authors clearly recognized, more easily aligned with universal moral precepts, then fitting the rest of the law into the structure of the Decalogue provided obvious rhetorical advantages.

There were good internal reasons for Philo to privilege the Ten Commandments in a manner unknown to the Hebrew Bible. But there is strong evidence that the Decalogue had already come to hold a special place in Judaism by the time Philo arrived on the scene. According to the Mishnah (*m. Tam.* 5:1), the Ten Commandments were recited daily at the regular sacrificial services when the Second Temple stood, followed by the recitation of the Shema (the prayer taken from the text of Deuteronomy, beginning with the famous words "Hear, O Israel"). The Mishnah is generally a reliable source of information about practices before the destruction of the temple, but for the practice of reciting the Ten Commandments there is additional supporting evidence. A Hebrew papyrus fragment known as the Nash Papyrus, dating to the late second century BCE, contains the text of the Decalogue followed by the beginning of the Shema. As this manuscript is ostensibly from Egypt (its precise provenance is unknown), it most likely reflects the practices of a private individual or local community, suggesting that the ritual use described in the Mishnah had expanded beyond the borders of the temple.

It is thus safe to say that the Christian focus on the Decalogue was not merely novel exegesis required by the new situation post-Jesus but was in fact the continuation of a preexisting Jewish attention to the Ten Commandments. Here, however, the story takes an unexpected turn. The Talmud—the commentary on the Mishnah compiled in two versions, one from the fifth century in Palestine and the more authoritative one from the sixth century in Babylonia—records that the practice of the daily recitation of the Ten Commandments stopped. (The reading of the Shema continued, and can still be heard at every Jewish prayer service.) The Babylonian Talmud reads: "People wanted to recite the Ten Commandments together with the Shema outside the Temple, but the practice had long since been abandoned because of the arguments of the Minim" (*b. Ber.* 12a). "Minim" is the rabbinic term for heretics.[10] The question, then, is this: What possible heretical claim could influence the rabbis to abandon the recitation of the Decalogue?

Here the version of this passage in the Palestinian Talmud provides the answer, and it should be a familiar one: "Because of the antipathy of the Minim, to deny their claim that these ten and no more were spoken to Moses at Sinai." The parallel with the early Christian emphasis on the Decalogue to the exclusion of the rest of the Mosaic laws is unmistakable, and has led many to conjecture that this talmudic ruling is a rare direct response to the rise of Christianity. Were this the case, it would be a remarkable irony: Judaism abandoning a ritual practice in response to a Christian argument intended to eliminate traditional Jewish ritual practices.

Though the influence of Christianity remains a possible reason for the demotion of the Decalogue in the Talmud, it is not the only one. Urbach points to historical evidence that in periods when Jews were persecuted, such as the reign of the Roman emperor Hadrian in the second century CE, it was not uncommon for Jews to conceal the public indications of their faith—going so far as to hide their circumcision. He surmises that there may have been a substantial number of Jews who gave up all the laws aside from those of the Ten Commandments—which, by virtue of being largely ethical, could be observed without obviously identifying oneself as Jewish—and that it was these individuals whom the rabbis had in mind when they referred to "the Minim."[11]

Whatever the root cause, the elimination of the Ten Commandments from daily Jewish worship was not easily accepted. Already in the passage quoted above from the Talmud, we see the desire of some Jews to restore the regular reading of the Decalogue. (In almost the next breath, the Talmud records that one of the rabbis wanted to reinstitute the reading in his local community but was dissuaded.) Indeed, despite the ruling of the Talmud, the Ten Commandments were read as part of the prayer service in various local communities well into the sixteenth century.

In Judaism, then, we see a long-lasting tension. On the one hand, we have the self-evident importance of the

Decalogue as the primary and only direct divine revelation to Israel. On the other hand, there was the desire to ensure that the Ten Commandments would not come to overshadow the rest of the law, as they had in Christianity (whether or not this was the motivating factor for the rabbinic ruling on the matter). In the end, the standard practice has followed that of the Talmud: the Decalogue is recited in the synagogue only three times each year: when the biblical passages in Exodus 20 and Deuteronomy 5 come around in the annual cycle of reading from the Torah, and at the holiday of Shavuot, which celebrates the giving of the Torah at Sinai. Even in these rather limited circumstances, however, the question of the Decalogue's special status remained. The great twelfth-century Jewish rabbi and philosopher Maimonides was asked whether a congregation could stand when the Ten Commandments were read, as had long been their custom. That this was, in fact, their custom signals that the Decalogue was seen as deserving of particular respect—it is not typical for congregations to stand during the reading of the Torah portion. And it was precisely on these grounds that Maimonides, following the lead of the Talmud, responded: "If we stand, we are making a distinction between these ten and the rest of the Torah."[12]

Both Judaism and Christianity assigned a fundamental importance to the Ten Commandments. For Christian authors, this led to the elimination of the other laws given at Sinai, and happily so—as Martin Luther wrote, "Let us leave Moses to his laws, excepting only the *Moralia*, which God has planted in nature, as the Ten Commandments."[13] For the rabbis and subsequent Jewish thinkers, this was precisely the outcome most feared. The internal discussions about the Decalogue can thus be read as ciphers for the broader understandings of the law, and the relevance of the Sinai event, according to each tradition. And while their conclusions could hardly be more different, both are grounded in a recognition that Sinai, and the law—however construed—was definitional for their respective identities and communities.

The Golden Calf

In the biblical narrative, the law-giving at Sinai is interrupted, and indeed almost canceled entirely, by the faithlessness of the Israelites. When Moses ascends the mountain to receive the tablets of the Ten Commandments, the people waiting below, led by Aaron, make a golden calf, thereby incurring God's wrath. Though Moses does assuage the divine anger, and the relationship between God and Israel is restored, many early Christian authors saw this episode as an opportunity to denigrate the Jewish faith. And, taking their cue from the order of the biblical text, they often declared the laws of Judaism to be akin to a divine punishment.

Justin Martyr, in his dialogue with Trypho, notes that there were righteous figures in the Bible before the giving of the law, who, "though they kept no Sabbaths, were pleasing to God," including all of the Israelites from Abraham down to Moses. But when the Israelites made the calf, and thereby "appeared unrighteous and ungrateful to God," then they were given the laws of Leviticus: "wherefore God, accommodating Himself to that nation, enjoined them also to offer sacrifices in His name, in order that you might not serve idols." Without the sin of the calf, therefore, there would be no need for the sacrificial laws that were unique to Judaism, and that Christianity had rejected. Justin goes on to point out that even this was insufficient to ameliorate the sins of Israel: "Which precept, however, you have not observed; nay, you sacrificed your children to demons" (*Trypho* 19).

Cleverly picking up on the identification of the law with slavery, Irenaeus wrote, "When they turned themselves to make a calf, and had gone back in their minds to Egypt, desiring to be slaves instead of free-men, they were placed for the future in a state of servitude suited to their wish—a slavery which . . . subjected them to the yoke of bondage" (*Against Heresies* 4.15). The laws that enslaved the Israelites, from which the advent of Jesus brought freedom to believing Christians, were attributable to the making of the calf; being thus enslaved was, Irenaeus suggests, a conscious choice on the part of Israel. Similarly the third- to fourth-century author and advisor to Constantine, Lactantius, claimed, "For when Moses, their leader, had ascended into the mountain, and there tarried forty days, they made the head of an ox in gold, which they call Apis, that it might go before them as a standard." Here Lactantius, in asserting that the Israelites worshipped not just any calf but the head of the Egyptian bull-deity Apis, seems to be picking up on a standard pagan slander, that in the temple in Jerusalem the Jews bowed down to a donkey.[14] Lactantius continued: "With which sin and crime God was offended, and justly visited the impious and ungrateful people with severe punishments, and made them subject to the law which He had given by Moses" (*Divine Institutes* 4.10). The law, like the punishments of plague and death, is the result of sin, and crime, and offense to the deity.

In line with the early Christian distinction between natural law and the laws of Judaism, we find in the *Constitutions of the Holy Apostles*, an anonymous fourth-century treatise, the following: "Propose to thyself to distinguish what rules were from the law of nature, and what were added afterwards, or were such additional rules as were introduced and given in the wilderness to the Israelites after the making of the calf; for the law [that is, the Ten Commandments, identified with natural law] contains those precepts which were spoken by the Lord God before the people fell into idolatry" (1.2). There is the authentic law, the natural law, and then there are "additional rules" given in the wake of the golden calf.

It is particularly telling that in this last text, but in Irenaeus and Lactantius as well, the polemic against Jewish law seems to ignore the fact that there were laws other than the Ten Commandments given before the episode of the golden calf, namely, the laws of the Covenant Code in Exodus 21–23. What these authors are specifically condemning, then, are the sacrificial laws of Leviticus, as Justin makes explicit (though, somewhat ironically, the Sabbath law that Justin directly mentions also precedes the making of the calf). It is the ritual and cultic practices of Judaism, including the kosher laws and the festival laws—presented in their fullest form in Leviticus—that are understood to be the direct outcome of Israel's apostasy. Judaism's most salient external identifying features are traced back to sin and punishment.

For many early Christian authors, the episode of the golden calf also revealed the inherently stubborn and faithless nature of the Israelites, and of their Jewish descendants. Origen put it most directly:

> For had they believed what they saw and heard [referring here to the miracles performed by God for Israel in the wilderness] they would not have fashioned the calf. . . . And observe whether it is not entirely in keeping with the character of the same people, who formerly refused to believe such wonders and such appearances of divinity, throughout the whole period of wandering in the wilderness, as they are recorded in the law of the Jews to have done, to refuse to be convinced also, on occasion of the glorious advent of Jesus, by the mighty words which were spoken by Him with authority, and the marvels which He performed in the presence of all the people. (*Against Celsus* 2.74)

John Chrysostom, the fourth-century church father, put it succinctly: "The Jews saw so many marvels happen before their eyes, yet straightaway worshipped a calf. Again they saw Christ casting out demons, yet called him one that had a demon. But this was no imputation against him that cast them out, but an accusation of their understanding who were so blinded" (*Homilies on Second Corinthians* 21).

Drawing a parallel between the sin of the golden calf and the rejection of Jesus allowed these authors to affirm strongly negative views of Judaism even while using Judaism's own historical and textual heritage to do so. The rejection of Jesus is equated with the rejection of God; failure to believe in

Jesus is labeled as apostasy. And if the Israelites were justifiably punished in the wilderness, so too they could, and should, be punished now. Moreover, Christians could now understand themselves as taking up the mantle of the true Israel—of those who kept faith with God when given a renewed chance. The Jews, by contrast, merely continued their ingrained trajectory of faithlessness. Leivy Smolar and Moses Aberbach, in their thorough treatment of the early reception of the golden calf episode, summarize this early Christian attitude: "By casting their gold into the image of a calf and worshipping it, the Jews had revealed their foolish, lustful, immoral, impatient, stubborn, unrepentant, unbelieving, murderous character, and abandoned forever their claim to the covenant of God. Furthermore, the sin of worshipping the golden calf had brought on its companion evils, which climaxed in the slaying of Christ and the persecution of subsequent generations of Christians."[15]

Perhaps the most disturbing, and influential, early Christian interpretation of the golden calf story comes from Augustine, who concentrates in this passage not on the worship of the calf but on what Moses does upon discovering it: burning the calf, casting its ashes into water, and forcing the Israelites to drink it. For Augustine, this is no punishment but something far more nefarious: "So there was enacted a great Sacrament. . . . What is this but that the worshippers of the devil were become the body of the same? In the same manner as men confessing Christ become the Body of Christ; so that to them is said, 'but ye are the Body of Christ and the members.' The body of the devil was to be consumed, and that too by Israelites was to be consumed" (*Exposition on the Book of Psalms* 74:13).

Augustine equates the Israelites' consumption of the calf with the Eucharist: as a means of becoming one with that which is consumed. He identifies the calf as a symbol of the devil; thus the Israelites, and their descendants, the Jews, become the devil. A reasonably direct line can thus be drawn between the episode of the golden calf, at least in Augustine's rendering of it, and the medieval (and later) depictions of Jews as the devil or his minions, complete with horns and tails. Augustine also opens the door wide to Christian mistreatment of Jews, on the same basis: "Let there be perceived therefore even now the body of the devil: this is what is coming to pass, he is being devoured by the Gentiles who have believed." This more righteous act of symbolic consumption is to be manifested in "reproving, blaming, accusing." The history of Christian persecution of Jews is foreshadowed here.

With this history of interpretation in mind, one may find modern invocations of the golden calf—often employed by cultural conservatives to denounce the ills of contemporary society, such as gay rights or abortion—to be problematically loaded with connotations of historical anti-Semitism. The trope of the calf is used to signal the wrongheaded will of the masses over against eternal truths ascribed to God. As Moshe Halbertal and Avishai Margalit observe in their important book, *Idolatry*, in "the modern rhetoric of idolatry . . . the category of idolatry is maintained, while what it is in opposition to changes."[16] As we have seen, this can be said to have been true for early Christian authors as well, who transmuted the physically realized idolatry of the Israelites' calf into Judaism's abstracted disbelief in the messianic status of Jesus. But every invocation of the golden calf, no matter how metaphorical, rests on the narrative of the Israelites in Exodus. And each contains within it the denunciation of a specific people, a condemnation that had astonishingly destructive historical repercussions.

It may be worth noting that despite the almost universal reading of the golden calf story as one of idolatry, the worship of a foreign god (usually related to Egyptian deities, as we have seen), the biblical narrative in Exodus is actually not so clear on this point. Most interpreters, and certainly those early Christian authors cited above, have read the making of the calf as a violation of the beginning of the Ten Commandments, "You shall have no other gods before me." Yet in the story there are multiple suggestions that the Israelites were not at all intending to worship any other god. When Aaron makes the calf, he says, "This is your God, O Israel, who brought you out of the land of Egypt" (Exod 32:4). The Israelites surely knew which god had rescued them. Aaron then goes on to declare the following day to be "a festival of Yahweh" (32:5). There is a strong case to be made that the law the Israelites violated in making the calf was not from the Ten Commandments at all but was the first law of the Covenant Code: "With me you shall not make any gods of silver, nor shall you make for yourselves any gods of gold" (Exod 20:23). The calf was not an example of worship of a foreign god but rather of the incorrect worship of the proper god. Such a reading, however, makes for far less effective anti-Jewish polemic—especially when the calf was used as the fulcrum point to separate the universal natural laws of the Ten Commandments from the specifically Jewish laws of Moses.

Conclusion

One of the most famous overlaps between Judaism and Christianity is found in, of all places, a discussion of the commandments of the Hebrew Bible. In the Synoptic Gospels, Jesus is asked, "'Teacher, which commandment in the law is greatest?' He said to him, 'You shall love the Lord your God with all your heart, with all your soul, and with all your mind. This is the greatest and first commandment. And the second is like it: You shall love your neighbor as yourself. On these two commandments hang all the law and the prophets'" (Matt 22:36–40; see Mark 12:28–31; Luke 10:25–27). A remarkably similar story is told in the Talmud of a Gentile who approaches the great Jewish teacher Hillel and asks to be taught the entire Torah while Hillel stands on one foot. Hillel says to him, "That which is hateful to you do not do to another: that is the entire Torah, and the rest is interpretation. Go and study" (*b. Shab.* 31a). Some generations later, the famous Rabbi Akiva would likewise claim, "The great principle of the Torah is: Love your neighbor as yourself." It is not for nothing that Leviticus 19:18 came to be known as the golden rule.

Hillel was a near contemporary of Jesus; Rabbi Akiva lived a generation or so later. Keeping in mind that Jesus was Jewish, it is not surprising that here, as elsewhere too, we see a strong resemblance between rabbinic teachings and those of Jesus. It is even likely that Jesus meant much the same thing as Hillel and Akiva: not that the golden rule is the only law that matters, but that if one law can possibly encapsulate the whole, this would be it. Note that Jesus is asked to identify the one law that is greatest, and

Hillel is asked to summarize the entire Torah in an instant. As Urbach correctly recognizes, "It was not the purpose of these reductions to minimize the observance of the detailed mitzvot [laws] in which the general principles find expression."[17] Certainly neither Hillel nor Akiva would have ever accepted any diminishment of the legal obligations found in the Torah; it is probable that Jesus did not mean this either.

Yet it is easy to see how, for Paul and other early Christian writers, Jesus's answer provided a foundation on which to construct a sturdy opposition to the observance of the majority of Jewish law. Jesus points here to two general principles, regarding each individual's relationship with God and with his fellow man, that fall squarely into the category of ethical teaching, and could effortlessly be construed as natural law. Nothing could be more appropriate for those looking to downplay the culturally and ethnically specific aspects of biblical law. Again, then, we can see that even where Judaism and Christianity find what appears to be common ground, it is undermined by deeper commitments—by philosophical and practical norms that served as markers of communal identity—that were designed from the beginning, for Christianity at least, as a mechanism for distinguishing one faith group from another.

What neither Judaism nor Christianity could avoid was the biblical fact that the Exodus story did not end with the departure from Egypt. It was not an Exodus from somewhere but an Exodus to somewhere—or, better, to something: to the moment of divine revelation in the wilderness, to the establishment of a nation, to the construction of a relationship between God and Israel. At Sinai, God defined new terms under which Israel was to live. What those terms consisted of, and how the people should apply them, became the primary point of contention between Judaism and Christianity, and largely remain so down to the present. But both faiths recognized the centrality of Sinai, and the law that was proclaimed there.

FIG. 5: An 1856 drawing of the Great Seal of the United States by Benson Lossing, based on Benjamin Franklin's 1776 description.

Social Formation and Communal Identity

As we have seen repeatedly, the Exodus was not just the re-demption of the Israelite people from Egypt—it was the creation of the Israelite people, born in the cauldron of Egypt and formed by the experience of divine rescue and the journey that followed. This formation occurred on multiple levels in the biblical narrative: with the difficulties of the journey, with the institution of cultural norms and beliefs, and with the arrival in a new homeland. Tying all of these together is a sense of hope, of a fresh beginning and the po-tential for a glorious future as a newly constituted nation.

Individuals have long looked to biblical texts as models for their own experiences. One may feel as oppressed as Job, or tested like Abraham. One may see oneself as an under-dog, like David when he faced Goliath. One may have a sud-den moment of faithful clarity, and share in Paul's road to Damascus. For broader populations seeking an opportunity to establish themselves anew, a consistent biblical model has been the Exodus story. Whether the community is physi-cally moving from one place to another or simply separating itself from the dominant culture around it, the Exodus story provides a memory and a symbol that can be adopted and used as a frame for understanding the present.

Appropriating the Exodus story in this way may seem a somewhat grandiose gesture. After all, taking up the mantle of the new Israel is both to cast others in the role of Pharaoh and Egypt—murderous, enslaving oppressors—and to claim divine selection and redemption for oneself. But the use of Exodus, or any biblical story, is not constrained by the closeness of the historical parallels. It is, rather, the natural continuation of the authentically biblical tendency to use history, and cultural memory, as a means of self-definition. What matters is not whether a given community is really in a situation similar to that of the ancient Israelites in Egypt. What matters, rather, is that the community is defining itself as something new, something unexpected, something grounded in shared experiences and systems of thought. For this, the Exodus story has always been the model and precedent. To claim a piece of that story for the present is to be conscious of a historical pattern, and to hope for the same glorious future that the Israelites looked to as they departed from Egypt.

In this chapter, we will explore a handful of examples of just this: communities, variously defined, drawing on the Exodus story to make sense of their own path forward in the world. All are drawn from a similar population set—essentially, Europeans living in, and in the wake of, the Reformation—but they are otherwise quite different from one another. Some did physically move to a new place; others stayed right where they were. Some looked to become a new nation politically; others had no intention of changing their governmental allegiance. Some engaged in a military struggle; others kept the fighting restricted to pen and paper. Despite these differences, all employed the Exodus story as rhetorical and conceptual backdrop—further evidence of the inherent flexibility of the Exodus tradition.

The Protestant Reformation

When Martin Luther nailed his "Ninety-five Theses" to the door of the church in Wittenberg, he could not have known that this act would come to be seen as the beginning of the Protestant Reformation. Even less could he have foreseen that he would come to be described as a new Moses, leading the true Israel out from the spiritual (and financial) bondage of the Catholic Church. Yet it was only seven years later, in 1524, that a broadsheet was published depicting Luther in just that way, with a (more Christ- than Moses-like) caption claiming that God has "saved us, through Martin Luther, with your Word."

Luther never took on the mantle of Moses for himself. But in his writings, and in those of some of the major reformers who followed him, the Exodus story loomed large in the background. Luther likened papists, with their stubborn refusal to listen to reason, to Pharaoh: "If one err through ignorance, he will be instructed; but if he be hardened, and will not yield to the truth, like Pharaoh, who would not acknowledge his sins or humble himself before God, and therefore was destroyed in the Red Sea, even so he will be destroyed."[1] Elsewhere he reminds his readers of the deliverance of Israel from Egypt, and the destruction of Pharaoh, before making the analogy abundantly clear: "As also, in this our time, he has graciously delivered us from the long, wearisome, heavy, and horrible captivity of the wicked pope."[2]

Luther's fervid anti-Judaism somewhat complicated his use of Exodus imagery. In a rather remarkable moment, Luther equates Moses with the enemy: "Moses and the Pope left us not in [our own] counsel, but restrained us by laws, and subjected us rather to their own will."[3] This clearly picks up on the post-Pauline Christian understanding of the law, especially in its equation of the law and slavery ("restrained," "subjected"). But it also turns Moses into a self-serving leader, rather than a true prophet of God; in Luther's view, Moses is both the liberator and the oppressor of Israel. (Luther was not entirely consistent in this; elsewhere he says that Moses "worthily performed his office as a faithful law-giver."[4])

Calvin also appealed to Exodus, and to Moses, in his calls for reform. In the famous *Institutes*, Moses stands as a counterpoint to the self-proclaimed authority of the Catholic Church. Because Moses was "not able to speak at all except from the Lord," so too "ecclesiastical power, therefore, is not to be mischievously adorned, but is to be confined within certain limits."[5] This is true not only of the creation of new doctrines but in the expansion of the papacy's spiritual leadership into the civil and political realm—what Calvin called "the right of the sword which they also claim for themselves."[6] Against this Calvin held up Moses, who took up the civil government of Israel, leaving the priesthood for Aaron. For Calvin, Moses was a figure of Stoic forbearance— though also a sinner, justly punished by being prevented from entering the promised land. In his sinful nature, Calvin found a model in Moses—a model that he took up, perhaps most practically, in insisting that he be buried in an unmarked tomb, just as Moses's burial place on Mount Nebo was unmarked and unknown.

Calvin's most thorough appropriation of the Exodus story is found, naturally enough, in his commentary on Exodus. There he does not stint from reading Exodus as a commentary on the struggle of the reformers against the Catholic Church. Like Luther, Calvin interprets the Pharaoh of Exodus as the prototype for Catholics in his day. When Pharaoh asks, "Who is Yahweh?" (Exod 5:2), Calvin writes, "We may remark a like madness in all idolators. . . . The cry of the Papists now-a-days is, that we are imposing a new God on the world . . . They seem to themselves to be sharp-witted and facetious, when they are scoffing at the novelty of our doctrine; though its truth would be plain enough, if they would only open their eyes."[7] When Pharaoh calls for his magicians to contest with Aaron and Moses, Calvin comments, "How many, now-a-days, among the Papists are followers of wicked superstitions under the pretext of simplicity?"[8] The concessions Pharaoh makes to Moses during the plagues, which Moses rejects as unacceptable, are likened to measures taken by the Catholic Church to reach a sort of temporary compromise with the reformers—which Calvin refers to as "a fictitious course."[9]

With the Church likened to Pharaoh, naturally enough the reformers are, if less explicitly, equated with the Israelites. In his exegesis of the midwives who save the male Hebrew infants from death, Calvin writes, "In these days, in which we have to bear similar insults, and are urged to despair, as if the Church would soon be utterly destroyed, let us learn to hold up this example like a strong shield."[10] At almost every turn, Calvin reads the text of Exodus as illustrating the oppression of the weak by the strong, including the story of the burning bush: "The bush is likened to the humble and despised people; their tyrannical oppression is not unlike the fire which would have consumed them, had not God miraculously interposed."[11] At such moments, Calvin hardly needs to make his referents explicit.

Similar sentiments were expressed by others: the Scottish reformer John Knox wrote, "The kings and princes which by power oppress the people of God and will not suffer that the people truly worship God as He hath commanded, but will retain them in Egypt, are brethren and companions to Pharaoh."[12] What Knox is calling for is not a physical Exodus but a revolution from within—or, for the more temperate Calvin, a hope that God would bring about the necessary changes. The Exodus story served as a reminder that right could triumph over might, and that God would not let true believers suffer oppression indefinitely. As we will see in the following sections of this chapter, it also provided a common narrative for the geographically dispersed and theologically distinctive reformation movements across Western Europe. Whatever cultural or conceptual differences may have existed among the reformers, they were united in their self-identification with Israel, and in their understanding of the Catholic Church as a new Pharaoh.

The Dutch Republic

In the early sixteenth century, the territory we now know as the Netherlands was, like much of Europe at the time, not a unified nation but a collection of loosely connected independent states. Reformation ideas, particularly those of Calvin, had infiltrated the area quickly, and found considerable support among the urban educated populace. The movement was met with strong opposition from the authorities. The Netherlands were controlled by the Catholic Habsburg emperor Philip II, who sought to impose a uniform faith on the region, executing hundreds of religious dissidents in the first half of the century, with more fleeing into exile. Because both religious and civil authority were vested in the imperial government, the reform movement inevitably came into direct conflict with political power.

In 1566 the conflict came to a head, with reform-minded mobs taking over Catholic churches with iconoclastic fervor. The following year, the Habsburgs reasserted their power, invading from their landholdings in Catholic Spain and instituting a Dutch version of the Inquisition. The year 1572 saw a new round of fighting, as Prince William of Orange, who had been exiled in 1566, returned and inaugurated a civil war that lasted, in various forms, for nearly a century—what became known as the Eighty Years' War. Over the course of the war, the battle lines became clear: the Northern Netherlands were Protestant, the Southern Netherlands Catholic. Eventually, the southern region dissolved into modern-day Luxembourg, France, and Belgium, while the northern area constituted itself as the Dutch Republic, among the first nonroyal states in Europe.

If the Exodus themes already prevalent in the Reformation were not sufficient, the particular historical circumstances of the confrontations in the Netherlands all but guaranteed that the Exodus would come to be the central narrative of the nascent Dutch Republic. Over the course of the civil war, Protestants living in the Southern Netherlands—around 150,000 people—moved en masse

to the north, not only replicating the direction of the Israelites' journey but also crossing the myriad waterways of the
Low Countries to do so. Early Dutch artwork regularly
portrayed scenes from the Exodus story, especially the
crossing of the Red Sea. Bards and playwrights took up the
theme with gusto.

The Habsburg emperor Philip II was a natural Pharaoh
figure. In 1612, a play nominally about the Passover event
drew the parallel clearly for its audience in its concluding
section, "Comparison between the Redemption of the
Children of Israel and the Liberation of the United Prov-
inces of the Netherlands": "The one bowed down Jacob's
house with slavery / The other, the Netherlands oppressed
with tyranny."[13] A popular song recounting one of the war's
crucial battles in 1588 likened the defeat of the invading
Spanish army—in which a thousand Spanish soldiers died,
many by drowning—to the destruction of the Egyptians at
the Red Sea.

An even more compelling biblical parallel was available
when it came to the Dutch hero William of Orange. William had once been part of the Habsburg nobility, before sid-
ing with the rising Dutch rebellion, enduring exile, returning
to fight anew, and eventually being assassinated in 1584. As
the historian Simon Schama lays it out, an obvious equation
was to be drawn between Moses and William, "who had also
'discovered' his identity while still a loyal member of the imperial nobility, who had also been forced by Pharaonic recal-
citrance into violent rebellion, who had also risked his own
life for that cause, and who, having delivered his people from
bondage, had died within sight of, rather than in secure possession of, the Promised Land."[14] William was depicted as

Moses in paintings and engravings, his portrait surrounded by images from the Exodus story. The same Passover play mentioned above contains the following lines: "O wondrous fate that joins Moses and Orange / The one fights for the law, the other beats the drum / And with his own arm, frees the Evangelium / The one leads the Hebrews through the Red Sea flood / The other guides his people through a sea . . . of tears and blood."[15]

The Exodus narrative was a way for the Dutch Protestants to see themselves as participating in a grand historical moment, reliving the biblical epic in their own day. In this respect, it served as a cultural touchstone, uniting and defining a people. (One may point to Rembrandt's remarkable, and remarkably large, 1659 painting of Moses smashing the tablets of the Decalogue: a symbol of the Exodus for a nation of the Exodus.) What made the parallel even more appropriate was that this was a moment of true national identity formation: out of individual states, a new republic was born—just as the story of enslavement and redemption became the unifying narrative for the disparate Israelite tribes. Any differences that might have existed among the Dutch before the revolt "were cloaked in a mantle of patriotic mythology in which God's bidding was disclosed just as surely as if it had been announced from the burning bush and hewn in tablets of stone."[16]

Yet among the fascinating elements of the Dutch story is that while the Protestants were rendering themselves as a new Israel, the Catholics were doing the same, if not on the same scale. As early as 1573, Catholic forms of worship were outlawed in the Northern Netherlands; priests were murdered. As Protestants fled north, many Catholics in the rebellious regions went into their own exile, moving south, into the royalist stronghold of Amsterdam, or abroad. One of these exiles, Wouter Jacobsz, wrote that he felt "strengthened by the miraculous liberation of Israel's children, of whom we were mindful."[17] Another Dutch Catholic author, Johannes Costerius, published a pamphlet in 1580, *Institutio Necessaria*, arguing that exile was the righteous path, invoking the oppressions of "spiritual slavery" and the Exodus as the appropriate models for contemporary behavior.[18]

It is hardly coincidence that Catholic writings echoed those of the reformers, especially Calvin. Reformation thought had suffused Dutch society for half a century before open revolt broke out. Yet it is also telling that the Exodus story was useful for both sides. As the ancient Israelites knew, and so many others have learned since, oppression breeds communal solidarity. It sharpens cultural borders. It creates the need for a narrative to frame and explain present desperation, and to provide hope for a more secure future. Whether the Exodus story is understood as part of the mythic and celebrated past or as a very present sort of experience depends on the vicissitudes of history. The Dutch, Protestant and Catholic, offer a vivid example of this.

Reformation and Post-Reformation England

Across the Channel, England was undergoing a similar Reformation experience. Beginning with Henry VIII's famous split from the Catholic Church over the matter of his many marriages in the early sixteenth century, continuing into the brief Catholic restoration under Mary I, reaching a stasis with the lengthy rule of Elizabeth, and breaking out in conflict during the English Civil War in the seventeenth century, the course of the English Reformation was anything but smooth. At each stage, one group or another held the high ground, and others were, or felt themselves to be, under attack—not only Catholics or Protestants but, within the Protestant camp, Anglicans, Presbyterians, and Puritans. The history is vast and confusing; for our purposes, we can focus on the specific question of how the Exodus story was variously appropriated by different groups, and to what ends.

Henry VIII's rebellion against papal authority may not have been grounded in a true belief in Reformation principles, but for English reformers it was nonetheless a breakthrough moment. As one wrote in 1543, the king's decision "intended such a thing as almighty God did when he delivered the children of Israel from the bondage of Pharaoh."[19] Henry's last wife, Katherine Parr, was also a prolific author—the first woman to be published under her own name in English—and in 1547, just after the death of her husband, she published her *Lamentations of a Sinner*, which included the following rather straightforward analogy: "Our Moses, and most godly, wise governor and King hath delivered us out of the captivity and bondage of Pharaoh. I mean by this Moses, King Henry the eighth, my most sovereign, favorable lord and husband ... And I mean by this Pharaoh the Bishop of Rome, who hath been and is a greater persecutor of all Christians than ever was Pharaoh, of the children of Israel."[20] The Great Bible of 1539, the first authorized vernacular bible, featured on its frontispiece a depiction of Henry VIII in the role of Moses (the

Great Bible was, unsurprisingly, commissioned by Henry himself). The Exodus story gave a broader and more cogent meaning to the otherwise rather tawdry beginning of the English Reformation.

The reign of Mary I was traumatic for English Protestants. She acquired the nickname "Bloody Mary" for a reason, executing 283 Protestants and forcing hundreds more to seek exile. Among the exiles was a group of Protestant scholars who made their way to Calvin's Geneva, where they produced a new translation of the Bible, complete with Calvinist commentary. The Geneva Bible quickly became the most important English bible until, and even for some time after, the creation of the King James Version. The first edition, issued in 1560, just after Elizabeth took the throne, featured Exodus imagery prominently and purposefully. The frontispiece of the entire text (as well as the title pages for Exodus and the New Testament) contained an image of the Israelites crossing the Red Sea, with text taken from Moses's speech to the Israelites: "Feare ye not, stand stil, and beholde the salvacion of the Lord, which he wil shewe to you this day" (Exod 14:13). The Geneva Bible also contained a map of Israel's journey through the wilderness. The map vividly illustrated the perseverance of the Israelites through trouble, and served as "propaganda for Protestant concerns at a hermeneutic level, for it and its fellow maps performed the important service of testifying to scripture's literal veracity . . . [a]s against Catholicism's alleged allegorical license," as Justine Walden notes.[21]

During the forty-four years of Elizabeth's rule, the Exodus story retained its potency, though it would come to be invoked in a somewhat unexpected way. Where it had once been employed against Catholic rule, the growing Puritan movement began to use it to criticize Elizabeth's religious policies. Elizabeth had long sought a more comfortable accommodation with Catholicism. For the Puritans, the Church of England retained far too many trappings of the papacy, especially the authority of episcopal bishops. In arguing for full Presbyterianism in the Calvinist vein, the theologian Thomas Cartwright accused Elizabeth of leaving the job only half done. He wished that she would follow "the example of Moses, who was not contented to have brought the people out of Egypt, but would very fain also have conducted them into the land of Canaan, that is, would gladly have been the instrument of the full and whole deliverance of the people." Cartwright credited Elizabeth with having led the people out of Egypt, but claimed that she had left them stranded in the wilderness. His plea was that she complete the task, and not be like those whose honor "is stained, and carrieth the mark of their imperfection by this and like exception, that, although they did such good things and such, yet they left also such and such undone."[22]

If Puritans found fault with Elizabeth, they were devastated by Charles I, who came to power in 1625 and instituted harsh policies designed to suppress the Puritan movement. In Scotland, where the first stirrings of rebellion occurred, the Exodus story provided hope: "I assure myself this church is in her journey out of her Egyptian captivity," wrote Archibald Johnston. "Let us even then read over the history of God's dealing with the Jews and their voyage, that we may learn to mark his dealing with our own Israel."[23] A member of Parliament drew the parallel between his present and "the bondage of the Israelites in Egypt." As

John Coffey astutely recognizes, "This was an incendiary analogy, for it begged the question—if England was Egypt, who was Pharaoh?"[24]

The return to religious oppression was described by many Presbyterians using the words of the Israelites when faced with their imminent demise at the Red Sea and elsewhere in the wilderness, when they longed to return to the relative safety of Egyptian bondage. Ironically, the more radical Puritan sects in England, who objected even to the authority of the presbyteries, began using the same image against the Presbyterians themselves. And, perhaps unsurprisingly, Presbyterians returned fire with the same accusation. The Exodus story was so pervasive that it seemed no other language was available for analogy, for argument, or for persuasion.

With the advent of the English Civil War and the rise of Oliver Cromwell as Lord Protector of England, Exodus themes were omnipresent. Cromwell became "our England's Moses," as one preacher declared.[25] Cromwell himself did not shy away from the identification but invoked Moses repeatedly in addresses to Parliament. Cromwell's son, Richard, who became Lord Protector after his father's death, was viewed by some as a new Joshua. Richard continued the veneration of his father as Moses, saying that Cromwell had "died full of days, spent in great and sore travail; yet his eyes were not waxed dim, neither was his natural strength abated, as it was said of Moses."[26]

Virtually every movement in seventeenth-century England, including many that were relatively obscure, drew on Exodus imagery in calling for change.[27] Some went so far as to view the entire history of England since the Norman conquest in 1066 as a period of enslavement like that of Israel in Egypt. Quakers, reacting against the Puritans, decried the identification of Cromwell with Moses, and declared virtually all of traditional Protestantism to be a form of enslavement. Apocalyptic movements acclaimed Cromwell as a Moses figure, but with the hope that an entirely new political system, akin to the law given at Sinai, was about to be inaugurated. And republicans, foremost among them John Milton, advocated against anything resembling centralized rule, deeply ingrained in English culture though it may have been. Milton wrote against the authority of both bishops and kings, saying that England's "sins were taught them under the monarchy, like the Israelites in Egypt, and have not been immediately unlearned in the desert."[28]

Of course, on this side of the pond at least, the most famous Puritans were not those who remained in England to fight alongside Cromwell but those who left for the promised land of New England. Already imbued with the Exodus theme from the context of the English Reformation, the appeal of the story was almost irresistible for those who were literally crossing a body of water to found a new civilization. William Bradford, who journeyed on the *Mayflower* and became governor of Plymouth Colony in 1621, likened the Pilgrims to "Moses and the Israelites when they went out of Egypt."[29] (Cotton Mather, the great Puritan preacher, referred to Bradford as a Moses figure.) John Winthrop, who would become the governor of Massachusetts, wrote in 1629, on the eve of his departure for New England, that his journey from the corrupted English culture was akin to how God "carried the Israelites into the wilderness and made them forget the fleshpots of Egypt."[30]

In order for the New England–bound Puritans to understand themselves as participating in a contemporary Exodus story, they had to draw two related analogies. Jonathan Boyarin writes, "There was first the ethnic-moral analogy, in which the Israelites were to Egyptians and to Canaanites as Puritans were to Papists and to Indians. There was also the geographical analogy, in which Egypt was to England as America was to Canaan."[31] These analogies operated at two distinct poles: the Puritans had to define both England and America, their point of departure and their destination, in biblical terms. The former was relatively well established, as we have already seen. Especially after the accession of James I and his suppression of Puritanism, it was possible to claim that England had come to be ruled by a new Pharaoh. It is the latter that required some conceptual work, and that had lasting and unfortunate consequences.

The Hebrew Bible is not particularly clear about the status of the Canaanites who dwelt in the land before Israel arrived from Egypt. In some places, such as the famous stories of Joshua, they are to be battled and destroyed. In others, however, the Bible suggests that God would have cleared the land of its prior inhabitants before the Israelites arrived. "I will send forth my terror before you, and I will throw into a panic all the people among whom you come, and I will make all your enemies turn tail before you. I will send a plague ahead of you, and it shall drive out before you the Hivites, the Canaanites, and the Hittites" (Exod 23:27–28), declares God to Moses. The Puritans seemed generally averse to the notion of taking up arms against the Native Americans themselves. The leading minister of the Massachusetts Bay Colony, John Cotton, wrote, "No nation is to drive out another without special commission from heaven, such as the Israelites had."[32] But they were all too happy to see God's hand at work in the diseases that devastated the Native American population, foremost among them smallpox. King James himself, in his charter for the colony, "The Great Patent of New-England," declared that "we have been further given certainly to know, that within these late years, there hath, by God's visitation, reigned a wonderful plague . . . in a manner to the utter destruction, devastation, and depopulation of that whole territory."[33] A pamphlet written in 1643 recognized God's favor toward the settlement "in sweeping away great multitudes of the natives by the smallpox a little before we went thither, that He might make room for us there."[34]

Here, perhaps more than anywhere else, we encounter the ethical complications of the Exodus story. Redemption and divine blessing are all well and good for Israel, whether the Israel of the Bible or the new Israel of the Puritan community; but they are mitigated by the resulting destruction of the Canaanites, ancient or contemporary. The Puritans seemed to recognize this, at least insofar as they put the fate of the Native Americans in God's hands rather than their own. In doing so, however, they effectively eliminated the Native American population from the narrative of the promised land, reserving it entirely for themselves.[35] The repercussions would be felt for centuries to come.

The deployment of the Exodus theme in the English Reformation, from Henry III to Oliver Cromwell to the Puritans of New England, highlights its remarkable malleability. That so many different groups, with varying experiences and agendas, should have all latched on to the same story is an indication that the narrative could not be constrained by mere historical parallel (though there certainly were such parallels to be drawn). In all of the cases described above, it is the combination of the religious and the sociopolitical that attracted the Exodus analogies. Each party looked to inaugurate a new way of living; each also recognized that nothing comes from nothing. There is always a conceptual Egypt from which a new corporate identity must emerge.

The American Revolution

The prevalence of Exodus themes among the generation of the American Revolution and especially the Founding Fathers, as they contemplated the meaning of their separation from England, is hardly surprising, given their Puritan roots. At the moment of independence, on July 4, 1776, John Adams, Benjamin Franklin, and Thomas Jefferson were tasked by Congress with the design of a new seal for the United States. While Adams preferred a classical allusion, proposing an image of Hercules, both Franklin and Jefferson opted for Exodus imagery: Franklin suggested a depiction of the Israelites crossing the Red Sea, and Jefferson one of the Israelites being led through the wilderness. These were merely the reflections of a broader trend to understand the remarkable historical moment of the Revolution as part of the divine plan, as a new Exodus.

As was the case for those Puritans who remained in England, the application of the Exodus story to the American situation required something of a logical undoing of previous understandings. As we have already seen, the Pilgrims who came to America in the first place believed that they were reenacting the Exodus and coming to the promised land. Yet little more than a century later, their descendants were able to speak of themselves as being back in Egypt—despite never having left their new Canaan, at least physically. A fundamental difference between the seventeenth- and eighteenth-century uses of the Exodus is that the American Revolution, uniquely among the movements treated in this chapter, had no significant religious aspect to it. Without any religious oppression to speak of, the Exodus narrative was applied entirely to political (and economic) impositions—which, to be fair, actually keeps it closer to the biblical Exodus story, which also contains no hint of religious persecution.

The aspect of the American experience that was first and most readily translated into biblical terms was also the spark for the entire Revolution: the British imposition of new taxes on the American colonies. It was but a small step from "taxation without representation" to something more dramatic: as Jefferson put it, England had undertaken "a deliberate, systematical plan of reducing us to slavery."[36] Once violence had broken out in 1775, the sense of biblical oppression only increased. In March 1776, the minister Elijah Fitch delivered a sermon in which he said, "The means, that our unnatural enemies have made use of, to bring and keep us under their power and control, are much the same which Pharaoh, Egypt's haughty Monarch used, and they have as yet had the same effect: Their schemes to oppress, divide, and then subjugate these Colonies, have served to unite our hearts, as one man, to cast off the burthens they have been imposing upon us."[37] A year later, another preacher, Nicholas Street, proclaimed, "The British tyrant is only acting over the same wicked and cruel part, that Pharaoh king of Egypt acted towards the children of Israel above 3000 years ago."[38]

Street did not shy away from broadening the imagery to encompass the entire Exodus experience: "We in this land are, as it were, led out of Egypt by the hand of Moses. And now we are in the wilderness, i.e. in a state of trouble and difficulty, Egyptians pursuing us, to overtake us and reduce us. There is the Red Sea before us, I speak metaphorically, a sea of blood in your prospect before you, perhaps." Indeed, as James Byrd notes, the American revolutionaries were particularly attached to the notion of divine war, and the fight against England as an expression of divine will. He notes that Exodus 15, with its verse stating "Yahweh is a man of war," was "the third-most-cited biblical chapter" in the century leading up to the Revolution.[39] Especially when the weather was involved—as when a hurricane destroyed a substantial part of the British Navy in 1775—the temptation to invoke the destruction of the Egyptians at sea was impossible to resist.

When the Revolutionary War had come to its conclusion, the Exodus rhetoric did not end. Indeed, the victory by the colonies was only further proof of God's favor, and cemented the narrative in the national imagination. Ezra Stiles, minister and president of Yale, delivered a sermon in May 1783—before the Treaty of Paris was officially signed, but well after the hostilities had ended—in which he began by recounting the Exodus story. He continued, "I have assumed the text only as introductory to a discourse upon the political welfare of God's American Israel, and as allusively prophetick of the future prosperity and splendor of the United States."[40] For the preacher Samuel Langdon, speaking in 1788, the Exodus analogy was pertinent not only for the redemption of the United States but for its imminent adventure in creating a new form of government. Drawing on the laws and customs established through Moses in the wilderness, he declared, "How unexampled was this quick progress of the Israelites from abject slavery, ignorance, and almost total want of order to a national establishment perfected in all its parts far beyond all other kingdoms and States! from a mere mob to a well regulated nation, under a government and laws far superior to what any other nation could boast!"[41]

It was only natural that the American Exodus story should have its Moses, and there could be little doubt as to who would receive that designation.[42] Somewhat unexpectedly, comparisons between Moses and Washington were relatively uncommon during the war itself, but they exploded once he assumed the presidency. (Ezra Stiles, preaching before Washington was elected, had compared him to Joshua, focusing on his military leadership.) Byrd gives a cogent explanation for this phenomenon: "For a new nation that had sworn off monarchial tyranny but had not completely lost sight of some of monarchy's advantages, Moses seemed to be the Bible's answer to America's need for presidential leadership. Moses was not a warrior-king like King David but a warrior-legislator, making him a 'safer' vessel for monarchial yearnings in republican society."[43] Thus, on July 4, 1799—only a few months before Washington's death—the pastor Cyprian Strong delivered a speech outlining the parallels between American independence and the Israelite Exodus, in which he said, "In the case of the Hebrews, God qualified and raised up Moses, as the leader of his people; whose wisdom and integrity, under the direction of Jehovah, conducted the Hebrews, through the stormy period of their national birth. In like manner, God raised up a WASHINGTON, whose memory will always be precious to the friends of the revolution; and qualified him, as a leader and commander of the American armies, through the bloody and arduous contest for national independence."[44] After Washington's death, funeral orations for him were replete with Moses imagery. "Moses led the Israelites through the red sea; has not Washington conducted the Americans thro' seas of blood?" asked Peter Folsom.[45] "A few steps more, & the israelitish nation would have pitched their Government in Canaan. A few steps more, and the American nation would have pitched their Government in the City of Washington," noted Ebenezer Gay.[46] As Timothy Dwight said in February 1800, "A strong resemblance between [Moses] and the hero of our own country is so evident, that the recital of it is become almost proverbial."

Redemption from oppression, deliverance in battle, the overcoming of near-impossible odds, and above all the manifest assistance and protection of the deity—the American experience of the Revolutionary War was shaped by viewing it through the lens of the biblical Exodus. Yet America was also forced to confront an undeniable and unavoidable complication in its adoption of the Exodus story: How could a nation so openly celebrating redemption from slavery continue to hold slaves of its own? This deeply felt ambivalence will be explored in chapter 6.

The Mormon Exodus

The seventeenth century saw English Puritans invoking the Exodus for their separation from the Church of England; the eighteenth century saw the American colonies doing the same for their independence from England; and the nineteenth century witnessed a group of Americans engaging in an Exodus from the United States to a new wilderness. The Mormon Exodus of 1847–69 entailed the mass migration of around seventy thousand people, moving primarily from Missouri and Illinois to the unpopulated region around the Great Salt Lake in what was then Mexican territory. Like every Exodus story, this one has its oppressions, its yearning for freedom, its promised land, and its Moses.

Though the Puritans came to New England in search of the freedom to practice their religion as they saw fit, their descendants were decidedly unwilling to allow the same freedom to Joseph Smith and his followers. Smith published the Book of Mormon in 1830; two years later, he was being tarred and feathered in Ohio, where he had moved to avoid the ill will that seemed to be brewing in his hometown in upstate New York. From Ohio, Smith was forced to relocate to Jackson County, Missouri, where, again, he and his followers were mistreated, their homes pelted with stones or burned to the ground. By 1838, the governor of Missouri had proclaimed that "Mormons must be treated as enemies, and must be exterminated, or driven from the State if necessary."[47] Smith and his people—now numbering fifteen thousand—made their way to Illinois, where they founded the city of Nauvoo. By 1844, Illinois was no more hospitable than anywhere else. Smith was denounced as a megalomaniac—admittedly, he was at the same time leader of the church, mayor, and chief magistrate of the local court; he had declared martial law in Nauvoo, and called up his private militia. Smith would die when a mob shot him in the jail cell into which he had surrendered himself.

From its beginnings, Christianity had understood itself as constituting a new Israel. So too Joseph Smith, in declaring a new revelation from God, saw the Mormon community as the new Israel. In 1831, when he moved from New York to Ohio, Smith said that God had told him to do so, "for I have a great work laid up in store, for Israel shall be served."[48] What was mere theological background for the reformers, the Dutch, the Puritans, and the American revolutionaries was very much at the forefront of Mormon identity. While for those other groups the experience of oppression brought out the identification with Israel, for Smith and his followers that identification was already present even before they found themselves in serious trouble.

From the moment Brigham Young determined that the Mormon community should head west, it was evident that this was an Exodus event. Claiming it to be so required no concerted interpretive effort, of the type we have seen in the previous sections of this chapter. No one needed to lay out how it was that the Mormons were like Israel, no sermons needed to be preached on the biblical texts, no parallels explicitly drawn. It was enough for Young to say, in October 1845, "The exodus of the nation of the only true Israel from these United States to a far distant region of the West, where bigotry, intolerance and insatiable oppression lose their power over them—forms a new epoch."[49]

Indeed, the Mormon Exodus was not understood as such only in retrospect, nor only conceptually. It was planned and executed explicitly along biblical lines. "We shall go as the Israelites," wrote one Mormon upon his departure from Illinois.[50] Young named the group with which he traveled the "Camp of Israel," and arranged them into divisions of tens, fifties, and hundreds, consciously echoing the judiciary units of the Israelites under Moses in Exodus 18. As Leonard Arrington notes in his biography of Brigham Young, the Mormon leader "unhesitatingly used ancient Israelite motifs in his letters and speeches."[51] The Mormon migration was a self-conscious Exodus from the start, and its destination was unreservedly compared to the promised land, to Zion. When Young had settled at Salt Lake City, he issued his call for the rest of the global Mormon community to join him, employing biblical rhetoric: "Let all Saints who love God ... gather without delay to the place appointed, bringing their gold, their silver, their copper ... to beautify, to adorn, to embellish, to delight, and to cast a fragrance over the House of the Lord ... for the time has come for the Saints to go up to the mountains of the Lord's house, and to help to establish it upon the tops of the mountains."[52] Recalling the journey of the Israelites, Young considered the Mormon Exodus to have done it one better: "The distance to their land of promise was but a few miles from the country of their bondage, while a great many of this people have traversed over one-half the globe to reach the valleys of Utah."[53]

Brigham Young was readily acknowledged as the Moses of the Mormon Exodus, and the role has remained his, as attested by the number of biographies with titles including the phrase "American Moses." Young himself recognized his status: "I feel all the time like Moses," he said.[54] One of the earliest biographies of Young, written in 1876, a year before Young's death, draws the parallels repeatedly and vigorously: "Scarcely had Brigham Young succeeded [Smith] in the leadership of the Mormon people, ere he was classed with the immortal law-giver of Israel"; "his name rang throughout America, and reverberated in Europe, as the Moses of the 'latter days,'"; "Brigham moved not as a captain at the head of a mere band of pioneers, but in every thing he well sustained the character of a Moses"; "Brigham was among them like an archangel of God. As a Moses he had led modern Israel in their exodus."[55]

Even outsiders saw the likeness. In 1852, only a few years after the settlement of Salt Lake City, a captain in the US Army Corps of Engineers, Howard Stansbury, came to Utah and produced a significant report about the region's geography and ecology and about its recent inhabitants. His description of Young is overwhelmingly positive, and entirely biblical: "Intimately connected with them from their exodus from Illinois, this man has been indeed their Moses, leading them through the wilderness to a remote and unknown land, where they have since set up their tabernacle, and where they are now building their temple. Resolute in danger, firm and sagacious in council, prompt and energetic in emergency, and enthusiastically devoted to the honor of his people, he had won their unlimited confidence, esteem, and veneration, and held an unrivaled place in their hearts." Just as Young compared the Mormon Exodus favorably against that of the Israelites, so too Young himself could be seen to have outdone Moses. Young made it to the promised land, built the temple, and was trusted and beloved by his people in ways that Moses could only have dreamed of.

The Mormon migration to Utah allows us to see what it looks like when a community does not find itself in a situation like that of the Israelites but considers itself to be Israel from the start. The Exodus themes in the Mormon experience were not the result of interpretive contortions but were intentionally constructed by the community and its leaders. Both Smith and Young recognized that they were actively building a new society—religious, political, and cultural— and they used the Israelite experience and identity as a way to unify and define the community of the saints. This was an Exodus from the top down, and their self-understanding has remained fundamental to the Mormon community's sense of its own history.

Conclusion

This chapter could well have included many other examples of communities using the Exodus story as the conceptual background for religious and sociopolitical self-definition— including, of course, that of the modern state of Israel. I have chosen to focus, however, on a relatively restricted cluster of populations, standing in a natural line of cultural continuity. Doing so allows us to see not only how the Exodus story took deep root in a specific context, that of the Reformation, but how even within that context it continued to be taken up, developed, and applied in a wide range of ways.

Some of the communities examined here read themselves into the Exodus story on almost exclusively religious grounds; others do so for purely political or even economic reasons. What constitutes biblical-level oppression is not fixed; nor, clearly, is redemption. Though we generally use the concept of the Exodus to describe population movement, that has never been a prerequisite for the appropriation of the biblical story. The biblical narrative is not really one of military triumph; yet an armed fight for freedom, however construed, is comfortably assimilated into the Exodus theme.

The Exodus story is not only flexible but capacious. The oppression of a Pharaoh, the leadership of a Moses, divine favor, the destruction of the enemy, the experience of the wilderness, the giving of the law—not only the entire narrative but each of these individual aspects are available to be used and interpreted in light of contemporary events. Which would come to the fore was largely determined by the historical contingencies of the moment. At the same time, the utility of the Exodus story was such that it often overcame incomplete or imprecise historical parallels.

The aspect of the Exodus story that all these groups share, however, is one that does not necessarily have an explicit biblical expression: the role of the Exodus event in the formation of a new community, a new people, a new nation, bound together through the experience of oppression and redemption, through unity of purpose, and through the hope of a happier future living as they wish.

What makes this particular set of examples fascinating is that they are like nested dolls, one emerging from the other. As it turns out, going through an Exodus experience does not result in a perfectly harmonious society. It doesn't take long, as we have seen, for the oppressed to become the oppressor, for the subordinate to become the dominant, and thus for a new community to arise from within the old. The rhetoric that once defined a revolution is turned against it; Moses becomes a new Pharaoh, Canaan becomes a new Egypt, and the Exodus story becomes relevant once again.

FIG. 6: Martin Luther King, Jr., at the March on Washington, August 28, 1963. Photo: CNP. Image provided by Getty Images.

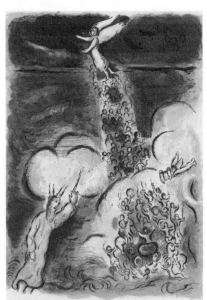

FIG. 7: Marc Chagall, *Crossing of the Red Sea* (1966). © 2018 Artists Rights Society (ARS), New York / ADAGP, Paris. Photo Credit: The Jewish Museum, New York / Art Resource, New York. Photo by Ardon bar Hama.

Exodus and Civil Rights

CHAPTER 6

As noted in chapter 5, the American Revolution, for all its glory, entailed a deep moral ambivalence. How could a nation that was formed in response to a feeling of oppression and enslavement, imbued with the rhetoric of the biblical Exodus, continue to engage in the practice of slavery itself? No one was more attuned to this problem than the American Moses himself, George Washington, who struggled throughout his life with, on one hand, the recognition that the institution of slavery was morally repugnant, and, on the other, the belief that his personal prosperity was wholly dependent on the continued use of slave labor at Mount Vernon. Though Washington was among the more enlightened of the Southern plantation owners, his ambivalence may be taken as representative of the nation as a whole. It was the basis for the rightfully maligned "three-fifths compromise" in the Constitution, and for the agreement among the Founding Fathers to delay any formal decision with regard to slavery for twenty years, so as to give the nation time to coalesce around those laws and values that both North and South could hold in common. At the time—and much more so in retrospect—the hesitancy of the federal government, and of Washington himself as its embodiment, was both inexplicable and unforgivable in the eyes of abolitionists. Even some who had once been among Washington's most ardent supporters (foremost among them Thomas Paine) turned against him as it became clear, as time passed, that he was not going to use his authority to stamp out slavery.

Though the debate over slavery in the United States would have arisen in any case, the widespread use of the Exodus story at America's birth threw the issue into sharp relief. In that discussion, the application of the biblical narrative changed in nature. What had previously been a "freedom for us" story became one of "freedom for everyone." Today, we are accustomed to thinking in these terms. Civil rights movements have so thoroughly and successfully appropriated the Exodus story that it is often difficult to separate the two. Yet we should also recognize the novelty of the connection between the Exodus and civil rights. Unlike the examples discussed in chapter 5, civil rights movements do not call for the creation of a new nation; they seek, rather, equality within an existing society. They seek full participation in the Exodus story that is already embedded in the national consciousness.

In this chapter, we will examine the many ways that the Exodus story has been taken up in civil rights movements throughout American history, and how the adoption of the biblical narrative contributed to the effectiveness of their message. We will also see that Exodus could equally be cited by those who opposed these movements. In order to understand how the preeminent narrative of freedom could be anything other than an argument for universal equality and civil rights—and to highlight just how revolutionary its use on behalf of civil rights actually is—we must begin, as we have so often, with the biblical text itself.

Slavery in the Bible

The book of Exodus makes perfectly clear that the enslavement of the Israelites in Egypt is an affront to God, and the impetus for divine intervention: "The Israelites were groaning under the bondage and cried out, and their cry for help from the bondage rose to God" (Exod 2:23); "I will free you from the labors of the Egyptians and deliver you from their bondage. I will redeem you with an outstretched hand" (Exod 6:6). The rationale for God's deliverance of Israel, however, is not any broad antipathy toward the institution of slavery in general; it is, rather, the preexisting relationship between God and Israel's ancestors, the patriarchs Abraham, Isaac, and Jacob. "I established my covenant with them, to give them the land of Canaan, the land in which they lived as sojourners. I have now heard the moaning of the Israelites because the Egyptians are holding them in bondage, and I have remembered my covenant" (Exod 6:4–5). What bothers God is not that a people is being held in slavery, but that the divine plan for Abraham's descendants is being forestalled by their bondage in Egypt. The affront is not to God's sense of universal human justice but to God's pride and power. The redemption of Israel affirms God's ability to bring to pass what was promised.

As we have already seen, Israel's release from slavery in Egypt is merely a prerequisite for their true service to God: "For it is to me that the Israelites are slaves: they are my slaves, whom I freed from the land of Egypt" (Lev 25:55). Even when service to God is construed as an obligation rather than a free act of faithful love, it is obviously an improvement over enslavement to a human overlord. But even this statement maintains a crucial specificity: it is Israel that is to serve God, not anyone else (the idea that all nations should worship Israel's God is a later theological development). And, therefore, it is only Israel whose enslavement by Pharaoh—or any human—is problematic.

Nowhere does God (or Moses, or anyone else) signal that all slavery is wrong. It is Israel's enslavement that is at odds with the divine will. In the Judeo-Christian West, it is common for the vast majority of the population to consider itself part of Israel—whether in the direct lineal descent of Judaism or as part of the "new Israel" of Christianity. But in the period of the Hebrew Bible, and in its texts, Israel was a closely defined group: a nation, yes, but a small one, surrounded by and living among non-Israelites. God's promise to Abraham, and God's covenant with Israel, was not universal but exceedingly particular. So too the biblical attitude toward slavery: we, Israel, are exempt, as the people singled out for divine favor by our national deity. The rest of the world is not implicated in Israel's redemption.

This is abundantly clear in the laws of the Pentateuch. These laws do not prohibit slavery across the board. Quite the contrary: biblical law recognizes two categories of slave—Hebrew and non-Hebrew. The first of these, Hebrew slaves, are essentially restricted to debt slavery: when an Israelite cannot pay his debts to a fellow Israelite, he must work to pay them off. Though this could well be unpleasant, it was, at least in theory, neither debilitating nor permanent.

Much attention is paid to the fair treatment of Hebrew slaves, with possibilities offered for financially redeeming them from their service and accommodations made for the release of all debt slaves at regular intervals. The principle is set out clearly in Leviticus: "If your kinsman under you continues in straits and must give himself over to you, do not subject him to the treatment of a slave" (Lev 25:39). Again, the claim that Israel cannot be slaves to anyone but God stands behind this sentiment: "For they are my slaves, whom I freed from the land of Egypt; they may not give themselves over into slavery" (25:42).

The treatment of the Hebrew debt slave is contrasted with that of the non-Israelite slave: "It is from the nations round about you that you may acquire male and female slaves. . . . These shall become your property: you may keep them as a possession for your children after you, for them to inherit as property for all time. Such you may treat as slaves. But as for your Israelite kinsmen, no one shall rule ruthlessly over the other" (Lev 25:44–46). The implication, clearly, is that an Israelite may "rule ruthlessly" over a foreign-born slave. Such slaves are pure property, inheritable over the course of multiple generations. Non-Israelites, not being party to the redemption from Egypt, and not having been singled out by God for special favor, are granted no kindness. They have nothing resembling civil or human rights.

The Bible itself, therefore—even in the law-giving that follows directly on the redemption from Egyptian slavery—hardly presents a straightforward argument against the institution of slavery. Rather, it assumes the continued existence of slavery. It even explicitly allows for the mistreatment of chattel slaves, mistreatment that is highlighted by contrast with the favoritism shown toward Israelite debt slaves. In light of the biblical attitudes toward slavery embedded in the Exodus story, the appropriation of that story for the promotion of civil rights is remarkable, and requires explanation.

Early America

As early as 1700, Samuel Sewall, a Puritan judge in Massachusetts, was taking a strong, if fruitless, stand against slavery in the colonies. His brief tract *The Selling of Joseph* is acknowledged as one of the earliest antislavery writings, and is organized entirely along biblical lines. Sewall picks up directly on the issue we have just raised—the distinction between Hebrew and non-Israelite slaves—and appeals to the advent of Christianity to counter it. "The Israelites were strictly forbidden the buying, or selling one another for Slaves.... Christians should carry it to all the World, as the Israelites were to carry it towards one another."[1]

It would take another three-quarters of a century or so for the abolitionist movement to really take off, but when it did, the Exodus story remained at the center of the argument. In England, the theologian and author Granville Sharp produced numerous writings against the slave trade, including, in 1776, *The Law of Retribution; or, A Serious Warning to Great Britain and Her Colonies, Founded on Unquestionable Examples of God's Temporal Vengeance against Tyrants, Slave-Holders, and Oppressors.* Like Sewall, Sharp focused immediately on the biblical treatment of Hebrew slaves and the impact of Christianity on the understanding of these laws: "Under the glorious Dispensation of the Gospel, we are absolutely bound to consider ourselves as Citizens of the World . . . we are absolutely bound in Christian Duty to entertain a Disposition towards all Mankind as charitable and benevolent, at least, as that which was required of the Jews, under the Law, towards their national Brethren; and, consequently, that it is absolutely unlawful for those, who call themselves Christians, to exact of their Brethren (I mean their Brethren of the Universe) a more burthensome Service than that to which the Jews were limited with respect to their Brethren of the House of Israel; and the Slavery, or involuntary Bondage, of a Brother Israelite was absolutely forbid." He continued with a warning: "The tremendous Judgments whereby this deliverance was effected (viz. the Plagues of Egypt) are so many signal examples of God's severe Vengeance against Slave-holders, which ought to be had in everlasting remembrance, to warn all Nations of the World against the unnatural and baneful practice of keeping Slaves." Noting the threat in Exodus 22 against the mistreatment of the vulnerable, Sharp wrote, "Mark this, ye African traders of this Island, and ye West-India and British American Slave-holders! For ye are all guilty of the like abominable Oppressions, and God will SURELY avenge the Cause of the Oppressed."[2]

In America, the same fervor was being expressed. Abolitionist Founding Fathers such as John Jay, Benjamin Rush, and Alexander Hamilton, along with influential writers such as Thomas Paine, argued against slavery as a matter of human rights, in line with the political and philosophical principles of the American Revolution. At the same time, explicitly biblical language was employed, unsurprisingly, by preachers across the Northern colonies. For these powerful speakers, who were finely attuned to the power of the biblical text, the disconnect between the Exodus language used to promote the Revolution and the continued practice of slavery was particularly acute, and they were not shy about expressing their opinions. "That civil liberty is of great worth, may be inferred from the conduct of God toward the Jewish nation," preached Nathaniel Niles in 1774. "We have boasted of our liberty, and free spirit. . . . If then it should be found upon examination that we have been of a tyrannical spirit in a free country, how base must our character appear!"[3] In the same year Levi Hart proclaimed that "the Egyptian bondage was a state of liberty and ease compared with the condition of these unhappy sufferers," the Africans seized in the transatlantic slave trade.[4]

The African American community was no less quick to adopt the Exodus themes so widely espoused by white American Protestantism. In 1774 the celebrated freewoman poet Phillis Wheatley, only twenty-one years old, wrote a letter to the Reverend Samuel Occum that was reprinted in multiple newspapers at the time. In the letter, she appeals to the Exodus story as the conceptual basis for abolition, equating American slaves with the Israelites: "In every breast, God has implanted a Principle, which we call Love of Freedom; it is impatient of Oppression, and pants for Deliverance; and by the Leave of our modern Egyptians I will assert, that the same Principle lives in us."[5] For Wheatley, America—which had already long been accustomed to understanding itself as Israel to King George's Pharaoh—was in fact Egypt, and it was the enslaved African Americans who were oppressed and crying for deliverance as the Israelites once had.

In 1794, Richard Allen, a freed slave, wrote in gratitude to white abolitionists: "You have wrought a deliverance for many from more than Egyptian bondage. . . . you see our race more effectually destroyed than was in Pharaoh's power to effect upon Israel's sons." To slave owners, he penned a reminder of the divine disapproval of slavery found in Exodus: "Excite attention to consider how hateful slavery is, in the sight of that God who hath destroyed kings and princes, for their oppression of the poor slaves. . . . We wish you to consider, that God himself was the first pleader of the cause of slaves."[6] Caesar Sarter, another emancipated slave, similarly reminded slave owners of the fate that awaited them according to the biblical narrative: "Be pleased to recollect the miserable end of Pharoah [sic], in Consequence of his refusal to set those at Liberty, whom he had unjustly reduced to cruel servitude."[7] The most remarkable moment in Sarter's brief essay is his reference to Africa as "a land that flows, as it were, with Milk and Honey." As John Coffey observes, "This was a startling reversal of the Exodus—if American Puritans had crossed the ocean or fought the War of Independence to find a new Canaan, Africans had been forcibly ripped from their Promised Land and transported to a new Egypt."[8]

Much abolitionist writing, from both white and black authors, was based in a notion of common human rights, or in a Christian universalism. But the Exodus story was most easily appropriated when slaves were viewed as full-fledged members of the (Christian) community of Israel. An important part of the Exodus identity therefore hinged on the conversion of slaves to Christianity. This was a matter of deep concern on both sides. Albert Raboteau, noting that slave owners were loath to convert their slaves, writes that, from their perspective, "to Christianize black-skinned Africans, therefore, would confuse the distinctiveness of the races and threaten the social order based upon that distinctiveness."[9] It was the non-Anglican confessions, primarily Baptists and Methodists (the latter founded by the ardent British abolitionist John Wesley) that pushed for both conversion and emancipation. And it was these communities that began ordaining black preachers, like Richard Allen, who took advantage of their religious and social position to promote the analogy between the African American experience and the Exodus story. Raboteau observes, "They mediated between Christianity and the experience of the slaves (and free blacks), interpreting the stories, symbols, and events of the Bible to fit the day-to-day lives of those held in bondage."[10] In this manner the black church in America was founded, out of the conversion of slaves and under the influence of pervasive Exodus imagery.

The slave trade was abolished in 1807, leading the freed slave Absalom Jones to preach his "Thanksgiving Sermon."[11] He took as his theme not the deliverance of the Israelites from Egypt but rather the call of Moses at the burning bush: "The Lord said, 'I have observed the misery of my people who are in Egypt; I have heard their cry on account of their taskmasters. Indeed, I know their sufferings, and I have come down to deliver them from the Egyptians.'" In interpreting these words, Jones pointed to the continued suffering of America's slave population. The Israelites, he said, "were compelled to work in the open air, in one of the hottest climates in the world; and, probably, without a covering from the burning rays of the sun. . . . Their work was dealt out to them in tasks, and performed under the eye of vigilant and rigorous masters, who constantly upbraided them with idleness. The least deficiency in the product of their labour, was punished by beating." The prohibition of the African slave trade, he recognized, was not the end but the beginning of God's plan for the eventual redemption of America's slave population. "The deliverance of the children of Israel from their bondage, is not the only instance, in which it has pleased God to appear in behalf of oppressed and distressed nations . . . The great and blessed event, which we have met this day to celebrate, is a striking proof, that the God of heaven is the same yesterday, and to-day, and forever." And further: "He has heard the prayers that ascended from the hearts of his people; and he has, as in the case of his ancient and chosen people the Jews, come down to deliver our suffering country-men from the hands of their oppressors." By situating the congressional act as a divine action, and more importantly by aligning it with the beginning rather than the end of the Exodus story, Jones employed the celebration of a completed act to look forward to a perfected future.

The Antebellum Period

Absalom Jones's vision of full emancipation as the inevitable result of God's intervention was not to be fulfilled for almost sixty years. In that time, as the abolitionist movement gained strength in the North, and slavery became increasingly entrenched in the South, the rhetoric of the Exodus story, deployed in the service of civil rights, similarly grew more and more powerful.

In 1831 Maria Stewart, a free Northern abolitionist, provided one of the strongest condemnations of America's continued existence as a slaveholding nation: "America, America, foul and indelible is thy stain! Dark and dismal is the cloud that hangs over thee, for thy cruel wrongs and injuries to the fallen sons of Africa. The blood of her murdered ones cries to heaven for vengeance against Thee."[12] Stewart goes on to invoke the Exodus story, leaving no doubt as to who was playing the role of Egypt and who was Israel: "You may kill, tyrannize, and oppress as much as you choose, until our cry shall come up before the throne of God; for I am firmly persuaded, that he will not suffer you to quell the proud, fearless and undaunted spirits of the Africans forever; for in his own time, he is able to plead our cause against you, and to pour out upon you the ten plagues of Egypt." Stewart recognized what Absalom Jones had intuited: that, though hope remained for divine retribution against the slaveholders and the societal edifice that supported them, the black experience of the Exodus remained frustratingly stuck at the moment of the Israelites' cry for deliverance.

In 1829, the free black David Walker published his *Appeal*, a literary contestation with Thomas Jefferson over the issue of slavery.[13] He begins the *Appeal* with a reminder of how Joseph and his family were treated by Pharaoh and the Egyptians, noting that while Joseph could rise to the level of vizier, second in command over all Egypt, "show me a man of colour, who holds the low office of a Constable, or one who sits in a Juror Box, even on a case of one of his wretched brethren, through this Great Republic!!" While Pharaoh gave Jacob's descendants the best land in Egypt, "where is the most barren spot of land which they have given unto us?" Walker makes his point clear: "to show how much lower we are held, and how much more cruel we are treated by the Americans, than were the children of Jacob, by the Egyptians." Herbert Marbury cogently observes that Walker's reading of the Bible runs counter to the typical Christian demonization of Egypt, and in so doing highlights by contrast the barbarity of the American slave state.

We can only touch on the manifold uses the black community made of the Exodus story in this period. Eddie Glaude, Jr., in his remarkable book *Exodus! Religion, Race, and Nation in Early Nineteenth-Century Black America*, summarizes the situation: "By the mid-1840s the metaphors of Exodus had indeed sedimented as the predominate political language of African Americans. The analogy had been diffused into the popular consciousness of black America. The ritual emplotment of bondage, liberation, and nationhood had been elaborated: the middle passage, slavery, and efforts to achieve freedom were understood within the narrative frame of Egyptian bondage, the wilderness, and the promised land. Exodus, in effect, was no longer the story of Israel but an account of African American slavery and eventual deliverance—the taken-for-granted context for any discussion of slavery and freedom."[14]

Exodus was also employed as the conceptual backdrop for a project inaugurated by white Americans: the colonization of Liberia by America's enormous free black population. The American Colonization Society (ACS) was popular in both the North and the South, as well as among the highest levels of the government, and some of its leaders were more than happy to take on a biblical role: one claimed to have "read of a Colonization Society that undertook three thousand years ago, to colonize in the land of their fathers, three millions of slaves. The President of that Society was one Moses."[15] Daniel Coker, a white minister who led the first ACS trip to Africa, saw himself similarly: "May he that was with Moses in the wilderness, be with us."[16]

Though still appealing to the unavoidable Exodus narrative, these sorts of sentiments employed the biblical frame in a way not intended by most African Americans. The colonization movement adopted the view that America had become a new Egypt, but rather than undo that identity through civil rights, it reinforced the notion that America was not the rightful home of the black population. It was an attempt to have it both ways: America was the Canaan for whites, and Liberia (or Haiti, or Canada) was the Canaan for blacks. The ACS was justifiably accused by some in the black community of both giving up on the fundamental dream of equality for all free Americans and, more problematically, failing to address the more pressing issue of slavery itself. A successful colonization effort would have left the Northern states devoid of blacks with equal status to whites, while blacks in the South were still living in the most horrific conditions. This was not lost on David Walker. His *Appeal* contained a screed against the colonization movement, couched in the language of Exodus: "How cunning slaveholders think they are!!!—How much like the king of Egypt who, after he saw plainly that God was determined to bring out his people, in spite of him and his, as powerful as they were. He was willing that Moses, Aaron and the Elders of Israel, but not all the people should go and serve the Lord."

What the colonization movement recognized, however —though perhaps unconsciously—was that the African

American appropriation of the Exodus story had begun to take on aspects of the national identity and social formation mode described in chapter 5. Glaude argues persuasively that, from the 1830s on, especially with the advent of the National Negro Convention Movement, the African American community shifted from a reliance on white support to a stance of self-determination. "In the context of a people stigmatized by the institution of slavery and racial prejudice, the call for them to debate and analyze the issues facing them . . . directs our attention to black agency." Glaude sees this as the natural continuation of the Exodus story: "The convention movement's call for black people to address their problems extended the covenantal convening of the nation that began with the emergence of the independent black church. Like the children of Israel, they had lived and were living through Egypt, and the experience had constituted them as a peculiar, perhaps chosen, nation."[17]

The continuing lack of progress with regard to Southern emancipation contributed to the emergent spirit of nationhood among America's black community. "Years have rolled on, and tens of thousands have been borne on streams of blood and tears, to the shores of eternity. While you have been oppressed we have been partakers with you, nor can we be free while you are enslaved," said Henry Highland Garnet in his "Address to the Slaves of the United States of America" at the National Negro Convention in 1843.[18] Garnet called for action rather than the seemingly endless patience that his brethren had exhibited thus far. In that call, he denied the Exodus imagery that had so long stood at the center of African American identity: "It is impossible, like the children of Israel, to make a grand exodus from the land of bondage." He foresaw that the end of slavery could come only with violence: "There is not much hope of redemption without the shedding of blood. If you must bleed, let it all come at once, rather die freemen, than live to be the slaves." Though Garnet's appeal drew on the increasing nationalism of the black community—speaking more in the vein of the American revolutionaries than in that of the civil rights movement—it was a step too far for most, including Frederick Douglass, who advocated for continuing with "the moral means" of addressing the problem. Yet Garnet was right: the institution of slavery would not end without enormous bloodshed.

The Civil War

"Jeff Davis is to the slaveholders what Pharaoh was to the Egyptians, and Abraham Lincoln . . . will be to us what Moses was to the Israelites." So said John Rock, a black abolitionist, in his speech "What If the Slaves Are Emancipated," delivered in 1862.[19] The identification of the American conflict with that of the Exodus story was obvious, even before the Emancipation Proclamation made slavery the central issue on which the war was founded. War, as we saw in chapter 5, especially when it involves issues of national and cultural identity, is a natural setting for invocation of the Exodus theme. The particularities of the Civil War, however, led to the unusual situation of both sides claiming identification with the biblical narrative, drawing on the same long-standing American self-understanding as the Israel of the Exodus, going back to the Puritans and the revolutionary period, although in a disproportionate way. For John Rock, like many abolitionists, it was the fight to free the slaves that echoed the Exodus story; for the South, however, it was the desire to escape the perceived tyranny and oppression of the North, and the end goal of creating an independent nation. Thus, even the national appropriation of the Exodus story was splintered by the Civil War.

Both sides were quick to identify the bloody battles of the Civil War with the crossing of the Red Sea (despite the fact that the drowning of the Egyptians was, presumably, a bloodless affair). The open warfare between North and South, and between abolitionists and slaveholders, which had been simmering for decades, had finally reached its final and decisive stage, just as the Red Sea was the site of the last (and only) direct engagement between Israel and Egypt. It was at the Red Sea that the enemy was destroyed for good; it was there that God was acclaimed as a "man of war," fighting on behalf of the Israelites. A Southern newspaper declared that Lincoln and the Northern army "will be buried in the Red Sea of defeat and annihilation."[20] Henry Ward Beecher preached in 1861 that the nation was standing at "the Red Sea of war."[21] "The oppressive traitors of the south are rapidly being overwhelmed in the Red Sea of blood," wrote a Lincoln supporter after his reelection in 1864.[22] Vice President Andrew Johnson, before he became the reviled architect of Reconstruction, announced to the black community of Nashville that he would take on the mantle of Moses "and lead you through the Red Sea of war and bondage."[23] As early as 1852, Lincoln himself had already foreseen the conflict required to free the slaves: "Pharaoh's country was cursed with plagues, and his hosts were drowned in the Red

Sea for striving to retain a captive people who had already served them more than four hundred years."[24]

Just as George Washington had been declared the American Moses, so now was Lincoln, and perhaps to an even greater extent. Washington's reputation had suffered as a result of his continued ownership of slaves at Mount Vernon; Lincoln, by contrast, had brought about emancipation, and at great cost, politically and, of course, personally. His assassination cemented his legacy as a new Moses figure, or even as one who exceeded Moses, for he "liberated more enslaved people than ever Moses set free, and those not of his kindred or his race," said Matthew Simpson at Lincoln's burial.[25] Memorials to Lincoln were suffused with the comparison: "He stands before us, and will so stand in history, as the Moses of this Israel of ours"; "our Moses who had only just taken us over the blood-red sea of rebellion"; "that Moses whom God had sent before them to lead them out of the land of bondage"; "the Moses of my people had fallen in the hour of his triumph"; "There lie the ashes of our Moses"; "our noble and praiseworthy President—our modern Moses." The references are almost endless.

In the early years of the war, however, abolitionists in the North were more likely to compare Lincoln to Pharaoh than to Moses. In part this was because Lincoln was the most powerful man in the country, and because those who yearned for freedom were not his own people. "The President has it now in his power, as had Pharaoh of old, to let the oppressed go free," read a statement in the *Liberator*, the fervently abolitionist newspaper of William Lloyd Garrison.[26] Lincoln's delays in proclaiming emancipation, as he attempted to center the war on the preservation of the

Union, were deeply frustrating. Many understood the horrors of the Civil War as the modern-day equivalent of the ten plagues, the national disaster that had to befall Egypt before it would relent in letting Israel go. The black minister Henry Turner, in 1862, wrote, "There seems to be a very singular correspondence existing between the war in the United States and the Egyptian plagues." He went on to render Lincoln as Pharaoh: "Abraham Lincoln . . . becomes the Pharaoh of mystic Egypt (American slavery). And however unwilling to comply with a dispensation of liberation, nature's God calls from heaven, echoed too by five million of the mystic Israelites (abject slaves) in peals of vivid vengeance, let my people go."[27]

While Washington achieved his Mosaic stature by fighting against the British, Lincoln's identification with Moses was almost entirely a reflection of the Emancipation Proclamation, rather than his military leadership against the South. Even Lincoln himself recognized that emancipation would be his Moses moment. He wrote to the governor of Illinois, who had pushed Lincoln to free the slaves, "Hold still and see the salvation of God"—the very words that Moses spoke to the Israelites at the edge of the Red Sea in Exodus 14.[28]

For the slave-owning South, of course, it was not the black population that represented Israel; they claimed that mantle for themselves. (And if Lincoln was the South's Pharaoh, the South had more than one Moses. The title was bestowed upon Jefferson Davis, John C. Calhoun, and Stonewall Jackson.) In New Orleans in 1861, a preacher proclaimed that "eleven tribes sought to go forth in peace from the house of political bondage, but the heart of our modern

Pharaoh is hardened, that he will not let Israel go."[29] Secession was the new Exodus; the independent South was a new Canaan. Secession was God's will: an 1863 statement by a convention of Virginian ministers, entitled *An Address to Christians Throughout the World*, attempting to put the onus of the war on the North, declared, "Let men discriminate between the downfall of an oppression when the oppressed have escaped, and a wanton effort to break up a good government. So Pharaoh fell, but not by the hand of Israel. The dismemberment of the Union by secession was not a blow at the government. It was for our own deliverance."[30] (Then again, the same statement also said, "The condition of the slave here is not wretched, as Northern fictions would have men believe, but prosperous and happy.")

In February 1865, Henry Highland Garnet preached a sermon before the House of Representatives.[31] Having declared more than twenty years earlier that slavery would end only with a violent upheaval—and with that violence having now occurred and drawing to its inevitable conclusion—Garnet turned his attention to the recent congressional approval of the Thirteenth Amendment, abolishing slavery. For Garnet, this remarkable decision was the moment when Congress had finally come to adopt biblical law, as written in Exodus: "Moses, the greatest of all lawgivers and legislators, said, while his face was yet radiant with the light of Sinai: 'Whoso stealeth a man, and selleth him, or if he be found in his hand, he shall surely be put to death.'" It was a decision taken only too late, however: "The destroying angel has gone forth through his land to execute the fearful penalties of God's broken law. The Representatives of the nation have bowed with reverence to the Divine edict."

Garnet shifted the identification of America, now that it had finally taken up emancipation. No longer was it Egypt, refusing to let the people go; it was now Israel, having heard the divine law but refusing to obey except in the face of severe punishments. "Great sacrifices have been made by the people; yet, greater still are demanded ere atonement can be made for our national sins."[32] Garnet looked ahead to the reunited America, in which the burden of slavery could not be placed on an Egyptian other but had to be borne by the nation as one. The enemy was no longer embodied by the South but was to be found in the abstract institution of slavery: "The nation has begun its exodus from worse than Egyptian bondage; and I beseech you that you say to the people that they go forward. With the assurance of God's favor in all things done in obedience to his righteous will, and guided by day and night by the pillars of cloud and fire, let us not pause until we have reached the other and safe side of the stormy and crimson sea. Let freemen and patriots mete out complete and equal justice to all men and thus prove to mankind the superiority of our democratic, republican government."[33] The Red Sea metaphor that had been used so widely to describe the bloodshed of the Civil War was reframed by Garnet. The military struggle may have been ending, but the true deliverance was still to come.

In appealing to the Bible, and specifically to the Exodus story, to justify abolition and emancipation, Garnet, like so many others in the North, had to carefully pick specific verses from the text. As we have seen, the Exodus story does not present a pure argument against slavery; therefore, a universal Christian ethic had to be applied to the law of the Hebrew Bible, or the slave population had to be equated directly with Israel, or the biblical text had to be reinterpreted entirely. Proslavery advocates, on the other hand, could pick out verses of their own, or simply point to the fact that the institution of slavery is explicitly permitted in the Bible, even in the laws given to Israel directly after their own redemption from Egypt. As the historian Mark Noll has observed, "All who wished to use the Bible for arguing in any way against slavery—whether by denying that the letter of the Bible should prevail over its spirit, or by denying that what the Bible seemed to teach it did not teach, or by denying that what the Bible in fact taught did not fully justify the system of American slavery—faced a double burden of staggering dimensions."[34] A Southerner did not require any fancy exegetical manipulations of the text; he could simply state, as one did, "that the relation betwixt the slave and his master is not inconsistent with the word of God."[35]

Among the most common proslavery arguments was that the black race was not to be identified with Israel but with Canaan. This position brought together the reading of Genesis 9, in which God curses Ham's descendants to be slaves forever—with Ham being identified in the Bible with Africa—and the pentateuchal laws regarding the treatment of Canaanite slaves. Even without the direct identification of slaves with Canaan, proslavery speakers and writers could handily counter any biblically based arguments against the institution of slavery in a universal sense simply by pointing to the fact that Abraham had owned slaves, that Israel was permitted to own slaves, that nowhere in the Bible was there any direct prohibition against slavery whatsoever. Noll describes the Southern perspective: "To propose for whatever reason that the Bible did not sanction slavery was to attack not just slavery but the Bible as well."[36]

Thus, while biblical interpretation was deployed as a weapon in the abolitionist fight, it was one that both sides wielded with equal passion and dexterity. The Exodus story was important for giving a shared sense of historical and theological purpose to the cause of civil rights, but it was not, as is sometimes proposed, a determining factor in the eventual outcome. Had the South won the Civil War, the Exodus story would have been held up as divine justification for their success. Indeed, at least as regards the literal reading of the Bible, which was the dominant mode of interpretation at the time, the proslavery side had a much better case. The fact that the abolitionist movement could make as much of the Exodus story as they did is a significant indication of how open the biblical text is to interpretive reimagining. It also reveals how deeply the Exodus story had permeated the American imagination and sense of national self: it was so pervasive that opponents as divided as North and South, abolitionist and slaveholder, could find themselves and their beliefs represented in and by it. As Lincoln said in his Second Inaugural Address: "Both read the same Bible and pray to the same God, and each invokes His aid against the other."

The Civil Rights Movement

The Exodus story continued to be pressed into rhetorical service during the period of Reconstruction and the decades that followed. It reached a new pinnacle, however, in the civil rights movement of the second half of the twentieth century. Frustration mounted at the seemingly intractable inequality of American society, expressed especially in the Jim Crow laws of the South. Calls for liberated freedom, for divine deliverance, and—at times—for direct conflict grew increasingly louder. The Exodus story had never been forgotten, especially in the African American community, but now it was reasserted as the defining metaphor for the black experience.

In 1953, Adam Clayton Powell, the representative from Harlem and the towering black politician of his era, delivered a sermon on the state of America, especially in the era of McCarthyism, and on the position of the black community within it.[37] Like Garnet, he identified the entire nation with Israel in the wilderness: America had received the law but had ignored it. Powell focused on the episode of the sin of the golden calf in Exodus 32, noting that Israel's leaders took two divergent paths: Aaron facilitated the sin, while Moses stood up to oppose it. Rather than take on the role of Moses for himself, Powell encouraged everyone to be a Moses for themselves. "Moses played his part," Powell pronounced—"What can happen when you play your part?" He went on to describe what happened after Moses's intervention: new tablets of the law and a new covenant. As Herbert Marbury puts it, "For those who heard the sermon that morning, the 'new law' held the promise that if they did their part, a legislative justice would supplant the old laws of Jim Crow under which they suffered."[38]

In one of his earliest sermons, in 1955, Martin Luther King, Jr., took a similar position. Reflecting on *Brown v.*

Board of Education, the Supreme Court decision outlawing segregation in schools, King preached on the conclusion of Exodus 14, when the Israelites see the Egyptians dead on the seashore. It was a moment of celebration, with the enemy defeated: "The Red Sea was opened, and freedom and justice marched through to the other side. As we look back we see segregation and discrimination caught in the mighty rushing waters of historical fate."[39] Yet King, and his biblically literate audience, knew that though one fight was won, there were hardships yet to come—an entire wilderness to be crossed before the promised land would be in sight.

This perspective was reinforced and made explicit in a new version of King's "Death of Evil on the Seashore" sermon delivered later that year, during the Montgomery bus boycott: "You don't get to the promised land without going through the wilderness."[40] As Gary Selby notes in his invaluable study of the biblical rhetoric in King's sermons, the boycott represented a new stage in the civil rights movement, one in which a significant black community "had united in a campaign of collective action against racial injustice."[41] An action that was expected to last only a week at most stretched for a year and a half, giving King ample opportunity, and ample rationale, to invoke the Israelites in the wilderness, moving slowly but inexorably toward Canaan, experiencing doubt and disheartenment along the way. The physical aspect of the boycott—walking—only contributed to the potency of the biblical imagery. "We have the strange feeling down in Montgomery that in our struggle for justice we have cosmic companionship. And so, we can walk and never get weary, because we believe that there is a great camp meeting in the promised land of freedom and justice."[42] Though the Supreme Court decision in the boycott's favor was a cause for celebration, King recognized the enormity and multiplicity of the challenges that still lay ahead, and expressed them in Exodus terms: "We know that the Midianites are still ahead. We see the beckoning call of the evil forces of the Amorites. We see the Hittites all around us but, but we are going on because we've got to get to Canaan."[43]

In a typically fiery speech delivered in Harlem in 1960, Malcolm X also employed the Exodus story, though for different ends. King focused on the patience required of Israel in the wilderness, hoping that the black community would find its Canaan within the existing structures of American society. Meanwhile, Malcolm X was branding America as Egypt and demanding that African Americans be given land of their own to build a new Canaan for themselves. He saw the obvious analogy with Exodus: "If the Hebrews in the Bible numbered only 600,000 in the land of their bondage, and God was concerned with giving them freedom in a land of their own, a land 'flowing with milk and honey' . . . then what about 20 million so-called Negroes here in America, who have the 'freedom' only to look for a job?"[44] In rejecting the wilderness motif, Malcolm X also called for a more literal understanding of Exodus, one that entailed not only freedom and equality but separation and independent nationhood.

Perhaps most striking in the comparison between King and Malcolm X is that these two black leaders, living in the same period and experiencing the same historical circumstances, could appeal to two different parts of the Exodus story to communicate two very different messages. As time went on, however, and as King's preeminent position in the civil rights movement drew increasing comparisons to that of Moses—and as the threats against his person increased—King too moved backward in the Exodus story. He continued to deploy the wilderness motif, especially, for instance, during the march in Birmingham. But King made increasing references to the beginning of the narrative, to the moment when Moses declared, "Let my people go." The night before his assassination in Memphis, King delivered a sermon in which the Exodus was once again the central theme. And, keeping with his message throughout, King used the biblical narrative to advocate for collective resistance by the African American community. "Whenever Pharaoh wanted to prolong the period of slavery in Egypt, he had a favorite formula for doing it. . . . He kept the slaves fighting among themselves. But whenever the slaves get together, something happens in Pharaoh's court, and he cannot hold the slaves in slavery. When the slaves get together, that's the beginning of getting out of slavery."[45] No longer was the black community in the wilderness; they were back at the beginning, still in slavery.

Marbury beautifully sums up the way that King used the Exodus story across his career as a preacher and civil rights leader: "In King's hands, the Exodus proved to be the preeminent inventional resource for addressing the needs of the movement at every stage of its history." This is testimony not only to King's rhetorical capacities but those of the Exodus story itself. "This underscores once again the enduring power and remarkable malleability of the Exodus within the rhetoric of the civil rights movement."[46]

Conclusion

It was not only the civil rights movement of the twentieth century for which the Exodus story proved so powerful and malleable, however. As we have seen, Exodus provided the conceptual framework for the struggle for equality in America from its founding to the present. Barack Obama recognized this in a speech delivered in Jerusalem in 2013: "To African-Americans, the story of the Exodus was perhaps the central story, the most powerful image about emerging from the grip of bondage to reach for liberty and human dignity—a tale that was carried from slavery through the Civil Rights Movement into today. For generations, this promise helped people weather poverty and persecution, while holding on to the hope that a better day was on the horizon."[47]

As a child, the first black spiritual I knew was "Go Down, Moses." I knew it, and even sang it every year, because it was included in the Haggadah my family used at Passover. The connection between America's history and the biblical narrative was obvious; less clear to me, at the time, was how the Haggadah captured another aspect of the civil rights movement: its ongoing nature, its lack of finality. The ritual of the Passover Seder was created at a time of Jewish crisis, when Israel was exiled from its homeland. Even today, when the state of Israel has been created and American Judaism is stronger than ever, the Haggadah still ends with words of longing: "Next year in Jerusalem."

Throughout American history, abolitionists and civil rights activists have returned over and over again to

Exodus—not only reaffirming its centrality but renewing its relevance in each successive era. Even as progress was inexorably made, each generation found itself still back in Egypt, at the shores of the Red Sea, or making its way through the wilderness toward the promised land.

FIG. 8: Arnold Belkin, *Éxodo* (1951). © 2018 Artists Rights Society (ARS), New York / SOMAAP, Mexico City. Image provided by the Museum of Latin American Art, Long Beach.

Liberation Theology

In 1971, Gustavo Gutiérrez, a Dominican priest in Peru, wrote *A Theology of Liberation*. The book crystallized a moral and theological agenda that had been developing in Latin America over the previous two decades and helped to popularize the term "liberation theology."[1] The movement emerged from a confluence of Marxist and Catholic thinking, and responded to the increasingly devastating and widespread poverty in Central and South America. In a sense, liberation theology can be seen as an outgrowth of the civil rights movements that we examined in chapter 6, the struggle for economic justice aligning with the struggle for legal and social equality. Yet the order of operations, as it were, is reversed. The biblical interpretation that was employed to support the cause of civil rights is moved to the forefront in liberation theology.

Liberation theology begins with a radical rereading of the Bible—at least, one that was radical at the time, though its arguments have now so suffused discourse about the Bible that it can seem almost obvious. The fundamental claim—that the Bible, and the God of the Bible, stands on the side of the poor and oppressed—is a bold challenge, not to Christian faith but to the structures and systems of power that promote Christian faith. Liberation theology speaks about God operating at the margins, rather than the center, and advocating for the marginal, rather than reinforcing the authority of the powerful. The Vatican rejected and even officially condemned liberation theology, in part for its Marxist tendencies, but largely because it entailed criticism of the church hierarchy in Latin America and beyond. Eventually, liberation theology came to be more accepted and integrated into Catholic thought. But some of the antipathy toward the movement can still be seen in the conservative Catholic response to the Argentinean pope Francis's unremitting focus on the poor.

If the civil rights movement required aligning the biblical text, or at least certain parts of it, with the rejection of slavery and discrimination, liberation theology entails a thorough reimagining of the meaning of the Bible. Rather than merely finding support for the poor in scriptural passages, it asserts that the overarching message of the text, from creation through the New Testament, is a declaration of opposition to poverty and social inequality. Poverty, as Gutiérrez defines it, is equivalent to death; the God of the Bible is the God of life. Poverty is thus an affront to God's will, and a challenge to divine sovereignty. Moreover, liberation theology holds that God not only defends the downtrodden but is actively on their side—what Gutiérrez termed the "preferential option for the poor," a phrase that has since entered the papal lexicon.

As a call not only for a new understanding of the Bible but also for practical social and political action and a reorganization of ecclesiastical structures, liberation theology has, over the past fifty years, become the dominant theological position for Christian theologians in Latin America. It has expanded to serve the needs of many other communities, not least that of black theologians and of the black church in the United States. In what follows, we will look at how the Exodus story—the preeminent biblical narrative of liberation—has been used by practitioners of liberation theology. As we will see, liberation theology has both mined the Exodus story for its sociotheological message and constructed a new interpretation of it.

Exodus in Latin American Liberation Theology

In this section, we will focus on the Latin American construction of liberation theology, exemplified in the works of Gutiérrez and J. Severino Croatto, an Argentinean biblical scholar whose 1978 book *Exodus: A Hermeneutics of Freedom* provides a full engagement with the Exodus story from the liberationist perspective.[2]

As noted above, praxis—the real-world application of theological principles—is central to liberation theology. In *A Theology of Liberation*, Gutiérrez seeks to bring traditional Christian theology down from the conceptual clouds and into the realm of the lived life. This is most apparent in his treatment of the idea of salvation, which he defines as "the communion of human beings with God and among themselves" (149). By defining salvation this way—as an eternal aspect of present human existence rather than as essentially eschatological—Gutiérrez brings the Bible to bear on the world around him. "There are not two histories, one profane and one sacred, 'juxtaposed' or 'closely linked.' Rather, there is only one human destiny.... The history of salvation is the very heart of human history.... The historical destiny of humanity must be placed definitively in the salvific horizon" (151). Anything that stands in the way of that communion, that salvation, is categorized as sin: "Sin is a historical reality, it is a breach of the communion of persons with each other, it is a turning in of individuals on themselves which manifests itself in a multifaceted withdrawal from others. And because sin is a personal and social intrahistorical reality, a part of the daily events of human life, it is also, and above all, an obstacle to life's reaching the fullness we call salvation" (150).

When present-day salvation is understood as inseparable from human history, it is only natural that the Exodus, the original biblical narrative of salvation, should play an important part in Gutiérrez's formulation. He begins his analysis by aligning the Exodus with creation: both are the work of God in history and the beginning of something new in the world. "Creation is presented in the Bible, not as a stage previous to salvation, but as a part of the salvific process. ... The creative act is linked, almost identified with, the act which freed Israel from slavery in Egypt" (152–53). Bringing these two concepts in line with each other accomplishes two ends. First, it expands the horizon of the Exodus event to incorporate the entirety of humanity. The specificity of Israel's redemption is subsumed in the universality of creation. Second, it sets salvation—liberation—as the very rationale for the existence of the world. If there is no Exodus without creation, then there is no creation without Exodus. A third conclusion emerges as well: humanity, in its present incarnation at least, was born not only at creation but at the moment of the Exodus. We live in a world governed by the ethos established at the moment of liberation from slavery.

Gutiérrez then makes clear the practical implications of living in a world formed by the experience of the Exodus. "The liberation of Israel is a political action," he writes (154). So too Croatto: "Have we paid sufficient attention to the fact that the first, exemplary liberation event, which 'reveals' the God of salvation, was political and social?" (18). This constitutes a significant break from the sort of spiritualized reading of history so prevalent in Christian thought, going back to Paul. Gutiérrez does not want to talk about any intangible spiritual redemption, or freedom from the slavery of Jewish law; he is interested in the authentic sociohistorical situation of the Exodus: "It is the breaking away from a situation of despoliation and misery and the beginning of the construction of a just and comradely society. It is the suppression of disorder and the creation of a new order" (154). On one hand, then, this is a move to more fully realize the Exodus story in human existence, to ground it in the shared reality of systemic oppression. Gutiérrez pointedly provides a list—which would be familiar to innumerable communities throughout history—of the mechanisms by which the Israelites were oppressed in Egypt: "repression (Exod 1:10–11), alienated work (5:6–14), humiliations (1:13–14), enforced birth control policy (1:15–22)" (ibid.). Croatto makes the parallel explicit: "There was also the additional intention to exterminate the race through infanticide—equivalent to the genocidal 'sterilization' that is practiced in Latin America under the euphemism of 'family planning' orchestrated by the North Americans" (18).

On the other hand, however, it is an innovative exegesis of the biblical text, one that relies on a thematizing of the Exodus above and perhaps even against its narrative details. Specifically, Gutiérrez does not seem to fully engage with the nature of the Israelite society that is formed in the wake of the Exodus. (Croatto, too, claims that in the Exodus event "Israel grasped a liberating sense of God and an essential value in its own vocation, namely, freedom" [28]. But, like Gutiérrez, he devotes all of his attention to the Exodus proper, and none to the complications of the communal legal codification that follows.) While there can be little doubt that Egypt was a land of "despoliation and misery" for Israel, there is reason to hesitate before calling Israel "just and comradely." In chapter 6 we have already noted that the biblical laws instituted at Sinai not only allow slavery as an institution but condone the harsh treatment of non-Israelite slaves. Yet while abolitionist readings of the Bible had to contend mostly with those non-Israelites, the perspective of liberation theology may be even more disturbed by the type of debt slavery that is described for fellow Israelites.

It is hard to recognize in the institution of debt slavery the sort of "communion of human beings among themselves" that Gutiérrez describes as the definition of salvation, at least not if that communion is dependent on fundamental social and economic equality. For some of liberation theology's more overtly Marxist practitioners, the Israel that emerged from Egypt was, indeed, the model of egalitarianism. George Pixley, in his liberation theological commentary on Exodus, describes Israel as "a classless society, a society of primitive communism."[3] Even without going to such rhetorical extremes, in order to see in the Exodus a move from oppression to justice—the type of justice envisioned by liberation theologians—it is necessary to overlook some of the most salient features of Israel's own divinely ordained laws. In his sharp critique of liberation theology, the eminent scholar Jon Levenson draws attention to the consternation the liberation theologian faces when confronted with the fact that the Covenant Code, the laws of Exodus 21–23, begins with the law of the fellow Hebrew slave: "This law occasions what is perhaps the greatest understatement in the long history of biblical interpretation. 'We are surprised,' remarks our Latin American liberation theologian, George Pixley, 'to discover that there were slaves in the new revolutionary society.' Surprise on the part of exegetes usually indicates an error in their preconception of the text. In this case, the error, by no means unique to Pixley, is that early Israel was a revolutionary society and exemplified egalitarianism and primitive communism."[4]

Levenson also points to the demand that Israel, having been redeemed from servitude to Pharaoh, now enter into the service of God. Gutiérrez, though without reference to Leviticus 25, focuses on the same element of praxis. Because Gutiérrez's overarching project is to align faith commitment with social commitment, he understands the identification of the Exodus as more than a political act: "Throughout the whole process, the religious event is not set apart. It is placed in the context of the entire narrative, or, more precisely, it is its deepest meaning. It is the root of the situation" (155). Gutiérrez points to God's words to Israel at Sinai: "If only you will now listen to me and keep my covenant . . . you shall be my kingdom of priests, my holy nation" (Exod 19:5–6). "The Covenant," Gutiérrez writes, "gives full meaning to the liberation from Egypt; one makes no sense without the other" (ibid.). Here his reading is fully in line with the biblical text. The laws that determine Israel's way of life are—contrary to so much Christian teaching—inseparable from the redemptive narrative of Exodus: "The Covenant and the liberation from Egypt were different aspects of the same movement, a movement which led to encounter with God" (155–56).

The manner in which Gutiérrez avoids commenting on the actual content of that covenant renders his understanding of Israel's new society—and, by extension, the new society he wishes to see in his own day—essentially aspirational. In the Exodus event, he writes, "the dislocation introduced by sin is resolved and justice and injustice, oppression and liberation, are determined" (155). He knows as well as anybody that such a society has yet to exist, from the time of Moses down to the present. By claiming this as the goal, therefore, Gutiérrez does more than simply express a wish for a better world. He invokes the necessity of a continuing human effort to bring about that world: "The liberation from Egypt, linked to and even coinciding with creation, adds an element of capital importance: the need and the place for human active participation in the building of society."[5] Croatto similarly writes that "the God-of-history is a God-who-comes. He is not revealed only in the cosmos, but above all in hope. . . . History emerges as 'project'" (8).

Egypt is representative of a system—what Gutiérrez calls "a sacred monarchy"—in which power of self-determination is withheld from Israel (and, indeed, from the population as a whole): "In Egypt, work is alienated and, far from building a just society, contributes rather to increasing injustice and to widening the gap between exploiters and exploited" (157). Injustice is thus endemic to the theopolitical system of Egypt, and, by extension, all such similar structures. True freedom—liberation—not only permits but requires active self-determination. The biblical narrative, of course, presents the impetus for the deliverance of Israel as coming first from God, in the remembrance of the promise to the patriarchs. But Croatto cleverly reverses the order of events by separating the historical event of the Exodus from the manner in which the Bible represents it: "The deep religious sense of the biblical worldview emphasizes the divine initiative of the process, but this is peculiar to religious language; it does not mean that this is the way it occurred historically. . . . The Exodus could have been, from an initial perspective, an intention that arose from among the Hebrews themselves. It was the 'event' that, from its very core, was manifesting a divine presence with all its implications (including the Covenant)" (20). For Croatto, more so than for Gutiérrez, the historical reality of the Exodus is crucial. By positing an authentic historical event, he can recognize the biblical narrative as a distinctive interpretation of that event—and thereby acknowledge the same possibility for similar events in his own day: "There are liberation processes in our world that seem disconnected from the Gospel, but which, little by little, assume a configuration bespeaking a presence of Christ the liberator. Examples are the peoples and groups struggling to change the situation of oppression on our continent" (ibid.). The Exodus and the modern world are historical realities, and in each we, like the biblical authors, can recognize the will of God at work even in ostensibly human ventures.

Gutiérrez writes, "By working, transforming the world, breaking out of servitude, building a just society, and assuming its destiny in history, humankind forges itself" (157). We may point again to the inherent tension with the biblical text in this reading. It is, after all, God who gives the law to Israel; Israel does not truly create its own society. Israel too is "a sacred monarchy," but with God, rather than a human figure, taking on the royal position. Gutiérrez gets around this issue in part by employing a new reading of the figure of Moses. Whereas in most of the sociopolitical movements we have examined in chapters 5 and 6 a single leader (or multiple single leaders) have been endowed with the title of a new Moses, Gutiérrez applies the Mosaic role more generally and generously. Again connecting the Exodus and creation, he argues that "to dominate the earth as Genesis prescribed" is to be called to "contribute to human liberation, in solidarity with all, in history" (ibid.). The raising of Moses to lead the Israelites is given as an example of just such a contribution to human liberation. By linking the two concepts, Gutiérrez effectively declares that every human, by virtue of having been created, can be a Moses. We need not wait for God to act, or for God to send another redeemer like Moses. "The mediation of this self-creation"— this is the importance of Moses: the ability of humans to define themselves as mediators of the divine will (ibid.). Given this perspective, it is not surprising that Moses is otherwise largely absent from Gutiérrez's treatment of the Exodus story. In part this can be ascribed to the fact that Gutiérrez may not want to get too close to asking the question of what it was, precisely, that Moses mediated between God and Israel, especially at the seminal moment of Sinai.

By eliding the content of divine law, Gutiérrez can focus on the notion that what God cares most about is what he calls "the liberating initiative." It is the act of redemption that signals God's will; the Exodus is "a political liberation through which Yahweh expresses his love for the people and the gift of total liberation is received" (155). Levenson may be right when he sees an undercurrent of traditional Christian anti-Semitism in some aspects of liberation theology, among them the evisceration of the laws on which Judaism was founded and continues to exist. Yet Gutiérrez, at least, seems less concerned with elimination and more with supplementation. The end goal is not to remove the laws; it is, rather, to introduce into our view of Israel a commonality with the present, a shared purpose in creating a more just society. What sets liberation theology against Judaism is, in part, the question of whether the blueprint for a perfected society has yet come into existence. For Judaism, one could argue, the answer is yes. The laws, biblical and rabbinic, exist as that blueprint, even though we remain in the process of bringing those plans to full fruition. Gutiérrez seems to place us still in the planning phase; this is logical enough, given that his theology is at heart a critique of the existing power structures: "To struggle against misery and exploitation and to build a just society is already to be part of the saving action, which is moving towards its complete fulfillment. All this means that building the temporal city is not simply a stage of 'humanization' or 'pre-evangelization' as was held in theology until a few years ago. Rather it is to become part of a saving process which embraces the whole of humanity and all human history" (158).

What makes the Exodus story so compelling for Gutiér-rez is not just that it models God's desire for liberation but rather that "the Exodus experience is paradigmatic" (157). More so than the Reformers, the Puritans, or the American revolutionaries, and much more like the slaves of the American South, Gutiérrez saw in the Israelite oppression in Egypt a close parallel with the lived social realities of his time and place. The Exodus story "remains vital and contemporary due to similar historical experiences which the People of God undergo" (ibid.). It is here that his liberation theology stakes its claim. Poverty is equivalent to enslavement and genocide: it denies to humanity the opportunity for self-determination, for participating in full communion with each other and with God—to "fulfill itself by continuing the work of creation by means of its labor" (158). The Exodus, and its covenantal aftermath, provides the fundamental framework for both oppression and liberation, and sets forth the proof of God's desire for a more just and equitable world. "Moses," Gutiérrez writes, "led his people out of the slavery, exploitation, and alienation of Egypt so that they might inhabit a land where they could live with human dignity" (260). To fail to fight for that human dignity is to negate the Exodus altogether: "To accept poverty and injustice is to fall back into the conditions of servitude which existed before the liberation from Egypt. It is to retrogress" (261).

At the same time, unlike any of the other movements we have discussed in this book, liberation theology takes an explicitly postmodern stance toward the interpretation of the Exodus story. Croatto puts this most clearly: "We wish to establish a hermeneutical perspective with a view to a 're-reading' of the biblical message of liberation on the basis of our experience as oppressed peoples or persons" (11). He does not claim that Exodus is, inherently, about the world he lives in: "We do not wish here to make 'application' to the Latin American situation." Rather, he begins from his lived experience, from his historical and cultural situatedness, and consciously reads that back into the text: "The facts of our world or our oppressed continent . . . must be, and are, prior to my interpretation of the biblical Word. Only thus is my interpretation eisegetical (literally, 'that which leads in') and not purely exegetical ('that which leads out')" (ibid.). By taking this stance, liberation theology makes itself available to each individual: "Readers will be able to orientate themselves in the interpretation of the sacred message on the basis of this hermeneutical effort, but they will have to 'say their own word' in extension of mine and confront the Word from their own situation" (ibid.). Moreover, liberation theology puts the onus of change on the individual and the community of the oppressed. Self-determination is both the goal and the means of achieving that goal.

Exodus in African American Liberation Theology

At the same time that Gutiérrez was publishing his seminal work on liberation theology in the Latin American context, James Cone came out with his *A Black Theology of Liberation*.[6] While Gutiérrez wrote out of the Catholic and pseudo-Marxist tradition of South America, Cone's work emerged directly from the American civil rights struggles of the 1960s. Having trained in a divinity school, Cone recognized that, even as the Bible was being used to speak to the

African American experience, the contours of biblical interpretation were still those of traditional white Christianity.
Like Gutiérrez, who called for a novel appropriation of the
Bible by the economically, socially, and theologically disen-
franchised, Cone promoted a black liberation theology that
was not borrowed from or dependent on accepted structures of religious thought. "It was clear to me," he wrote,
"that what was needed was a fresh start in theology, a new
way of doing it that would arise out of the black struggle for
justice and in no way would be dependent upon the approval of white academics in religion" (xvii).

Cone, again like Gutiérrez, saw in traditional theology
the hegemony of the dominant culture: "The time had
come to expose white theology for what it was: a racist,
theological justification of the status quo" (xviii). Cone's
passion openly channeled the attitude of the more radical
aspects of the civil rights movement: "My style of doing
theology was influenced more by Malcolm X than by Martin Luther King, Jr." (xix). Just as Malcolm X had railed
against what he saw as King's accommodationism to white
authority, so too Cone promoted not an adjustment of traditional theology but a radical break with it—a "fresh
start" altogether.

Though Cone had not read Gutiérrez when he wrote his
book, many of the basic ideas are easily recognizable. He begins by stating openly, "Christian theology is a theology of
liberation. . . . There can be no Christian theology that is not
identified unreservedly with those who are humiliated and
abused. In fact, theology ceases to be a theology of the gospel when it fails to arise out of the community of the oppressed" (1). In these few words, Cone captures the essence

of liberation theology: the notion that the Bible is not only on the side of the oppressed but it must be reclaimed and read by—and in light of—the oppressed. The basis for this claim is found, as we might expect, in the oppression and redemption of the Exodus story: "It is impossible to speak of the God of Israelite history . . . without recognizing that God is the God of and for those who labor and are over-laden" (ibid.).

For Cone, the very definition of God is grounded in the Exodus: "By delivering this people from Egyptian bondage and inaugurating the covenant on the basis of that historical event, God is revealed as the God of the oppressed, involved in their history, liberating them from human bondage" (2). And, as this is God's true and inherent nature, what was exhibited in the ancient past must be brought to bear on the present: "The task of theology, then, is to explicate the meaning of God's liberating activity so that those who labor under enslaving powers will see that the forces of liberation are the very activity of God" (3). Like Gutiérrez, Cone brings the understanding of God out of a distant and ineffable realm and into the real world: "Christian theology is never just a rational study of the being of God. Rather it is a study of God's liberating activity in the world, God's activity in behalf of the oppressed" (ibid.). Here the challenge to traditional theology is plain: the innumerable tomes written in the white Western Christian tradition about the nature of the deity are just so many words. "Whatever theology says about God and the world must arise out of its sole reason for existence as a discipline: to assist the oppressed in their liberation" (4). Theology belongs in the streets, not in the ivory tower: "If God is not involved in human history, then all theology is useless, and Christianity itself is a mockery, a hollow, meaningless diversion" (6–7).

The most striking innovation in Cone's liberation theology is its unrelenting focus on race. While this played a part for Gutiérrez and other Latin American theologians, they largely targeted distinctions of class and economic status. Cone, however, writing in the context of the United States and the civil rights movement, recognizes that race, and racism, undergirds all of the nation's present and historical socioeconomic injustices: "The extermination of Amerindians, the persecution of Jews, the oppression of Mexican-Americans, and every other conceivable inhumanity done in the name of God and country—these brutalities can be analyzed in terms of the white American inability to recognize humanity in persons of color" (8). Thus Cone's concept of liberation theology is broader than that found in Gutiérrez: it encompasses not only poverty but any and all oppression at the hands of white power.

Not surprisingly, Cone uses the language of slavery, rather than poverty, to express this all-encompassing oppression. But his formulation is similar: slavery is defined as "the suppression of everything creative" (92). Just as Gutiérrez argued that poverty prevents people from achieving their divinely granted potential, Cone states that "to be human is to be free, and to be free is to be human. . . . To be free means that human beings are not an object, and they will not let others treat them as an 'it'" (92, 94). Moreover, "being human means being against evil by joining sides with those who are the victims of evil" (93)—thus only those involved in the fight for freedom deserve to be called fully human. In a move strikingly parallel to that of Gutiérrez,

Cone connects the task of dominion over the earth granted to mankind in Genesis 1 with the Exodus: "The task includes participation in the freedom of God in the liberation of God's people" (ibid.). The created human is the liberating human: "It is the biblical concept of the image of God that makes black rebellion in America human. When black persons affirm their freedom in God, they must say no to white racists. By saying no, they say yes to God and their blackness, affirming at the same time the inhumanity of the white neighbor who insists on playing God" (99). Blackness, liberation, and humanity are on one side; whiteness, slavery—writ large—and inhumanity are on the other. To be black is to be the Israel of the Exodus; to be white is to be Pharaoh.

While Cone's theology may entail a more strident and confrontational style of liberation—"it is blacks telling whites where to get off, and a willingness to accept the consequences" (48)—it is still a call for communal action, and one that is still based in the Exodus story. To get there, Cone, like Croatto, draws out the relationship between history and faith, between an event and its interpretation. The historical fact of the Exodus stands on its own, "but only those with the faith of Israel would know that those liberative events were God's self-revelation. . . . Faith, then, is the existential recognition of a situation of oppression and a participation in God's liberation" (50). It is the participatory aspect that is brought to the fore. For Cone, faith is not the deliberative reflection on God but "the response of the community to God's act of liberation. It means saying yes to God and no to oppressors" (ibid.).

With faith construed as resistance to oppression—as "the community's perception of its being and the willingness to fight against nonbeing" (50)—there is an implicit call for resistance among those who consider themselves faithful. Those who resist, whether explicitly in the name of faith or otherwise, are implicated in the liberative project of the God of the Bible. It was Israel's communal interpretation of the Exodus as divine liberation that gave it power; so too Cone interprets the resistance exhibited by African Americans as part of the divine plan: "How could we speak about God's revelation in the exodus, the conquest of Palestine, the role of the judges in Israel without seeing parallels in black history?" (ibid.). Citing Nat Turner, Denmark Vesey, and Malcolm X, he declares, "They are the black judges endowed with the spirit of Yahweh for the sole purpose of creating a spirit of freedom among their people" (51). Note that even when singling out individuals, Cone still brings the focus back to the community—it is at the communal level that liberation must be felt and put into action.

Communal failure to resist is not just a failure of will; it is the definition of sin: "To be in sin has nothing to do with disobeying laws that are alien to the community's existence. Quite the contrary, failure to destroy the powers that seek to enforce alien laws on the community is to be in a state of sin. It is incumbent on all members of the community to define their existence according to the community's essence and to defend the community against that which seeks to destroy it" (113). Here Cone refers us to the covenant between God and Israel made at Sinai. Implicitly recognizing that the covenant is dependent on God's redemptive act, Cone writes that the covenant "is the agreement between Yahweh and his people that Yahweh would continue a liberative presence if Israel would define its existence as a community on the basis of divine liberation" (112). This is a softer way of putting the obligatory nature of the covenant: because God freed Israel, they are required to obey. Yet it also impressively highlights the notion that all the laws are grounded not only in obedience but in obedience to a God of liberation. Thus disobedience is a denial of this definition of the deity: "Sin, then, is the failure of Israel to recognize the liberating work of God. It is believing that liberation is not the definition of being in the world" (ibid.). Cone's treatment of sin, not as an individual's rebellion against the content of the law but as a community's failure to live into the rationale behind the law, is powerful and requires each individual to work on behalf of the whole: "To revolt against the community's reason for being is to deny the reality of the community itself" (ibid.).

Fundamental to Cone's thinking, as with that of Gutiérrez and liberation theology more broadly, is the argument that none of these categories—salvation, liberation, faith, sin—are intellectual or spiritual. They are real, practical, and historical. In his 1975 volume *God of the Oppressed*, Cone elaborates on this central issue: "Whatever may be said about the biblical faith and black faith derived from Scriptures, neither was based on a feeling of inwardness separated from historical experience. Both Israel and later the black community took history seriously and continued to test the validity of their faith in the context of historical struggle."[7] In this manner, Cone negates the prevailing tendency to separate the reality of the modern lived experience from the spiritualized or allegorized meaning of the biblical narrative. The lessons to be drawn from the Bible must always be relevant to the lived world of the present:

"Theologians must make the gospel clear in a particular social context so that God's people will know that their struggle for freedom is God's struggle too."[8] It is here most of all
that the Exodus story is crucial for Cone's liberation theology: as proof of God's historical intervention on the side of
the wronged. "The victory over evil is certain because God
has taken up the cause of the oppressed, promising today
what was promised to the people of Israel while they were
yet slaves in Egypt."[9]

Cone's liberation theology is as openly culturally situated as that of Croatto. In the preface to the revised edition of *God of the Oppressed*, he writes, "The black experience and the Bible together in dialectical tension serve as
my point of departure today and yesterday. The order is
significant. I am black first—and everything else comes
after that. This means that I read the Bible through the lens
of a black tradition of struggle and not as the objective
Word of God."[10] In this way Cone can both particularize
his reading of the Bible and simultaneously make it available to all. "No experience can take precedence over
the truth revealed in black people's struggle for full
humanity"—the particular. "The same rule of faith should
be used by all oppressed people as they reflect on God in
their struggle for wholeness"—the universal.[11] The Exodus
story, therefore, is understood not so much as a story about
Israel but as one about God. What looks like national or
cultural specificity—Israel is chosen for redemption while
others are not—is in fact a model for understanding God's
desire for human liberation, applied to all peoples in all
places, whether or not they identify with Israel.

CHAPTER 7

The Reach of Liberation Theology

In light of the universalistic nature of liberation theology, it is no surprise that its impact has been felt far beyond the Latin American and African American cultural contexts. It is impossible in this space to do justice to the scope of liberation theology's influence, so the following examples are meant only to be representative, not exhaustive. In this section we will briefly explore three quite different applications of liberation theology and the Exodus theme—including one that presents an important challenge to traditional formulations.

In his book *The Book of Exodus and Dalit Liberation*, D. Manohar Chandra Prasad, a priest in the Church of South India, brings the Exodus story and liberation theology to bear on the struggles of the Christian Dalit, the lowest caste of traditional society in India.[12] Like Cone and Gutiérrez, Prasad deploys his liberationist reading of Exodus as a call to action: "to understand the closeness of Exodus events to the present day Dalit liberation struggles, so as to empower Dalits through ideological, theological and spiritual resources in their warfare against the oppressors in the Indian context" (76). Dalit identification with the Exodus story, and its implications for God's liberative desires, is required, Prasad argues, in order both to ground their struggle ideologically and, more basically, to make them aware of the liberationist reading of Exodus and how it might apply to their situation.

Centuries, even millennia, of Dalit oppression by upper-caste Indians make the analogies with Israel's slavery in

Egypt easy to draw. "Caste society has forced [Dalits] to be the virtual slaves of the Hindu Brahmanical society. . . . For thousands of years Dalits have been used to build the wealth of the upper caste Hindu society, like Israel who built Pitom and Ramses. . . . Like in the land of Egypt, the laws of the land were made to make the life of the Dalits and poor more bitter and miserable" (88). Prasad makes a strong case that the Dalit have it even worse than the Israelites did: "Dalits have been suffering bondage and slavery for more than 3500 years" (90).

"The cry of the innocent blood and the oppressed," Prasad writes of Exodus, "invoke God's response and his mighty act against the oppressors. . . . Blood in the Bible is shed to release the oppressed. Blood is life and Dalits have been shedding their blood in the casteist Hindu society for centuries. They are continuously making their cry against the treacherous Hindu upper caste rules, and beseeching God to intervene on behalf of their total liberation" (79). The caste system, like economic injustice in Latin America and racism in the United States—and like slavery in Egypt—treats the Dalit as less than fully human. "Yahweh identifies with those who never had their own identity in the world of exploiters. Through God's identity the no-people also will gain identity" (83).

The cultural silencing of Dalit voices provides another locus of overlap with the Exodus story. Prasad describes the Israelites as having been "made mute" by suffering; the call of Moses at the burning bush is thus the initiating moment for both divine communication with Israel and for a new period of Israel's communication with God: "The oppressed were called by God to communicate their oppressed conditions" (87). Prasad uses liberationist readings to empower the Dalit community to enter into a new phase of their existence: "God was equipping the unspeakable mute nation through Moses. The purpose of God's revelation was to reveal the situation of Dalits" (88). At stake here, at least in part, is the role that Christian missionary work in India plays in bringing liberationist ideas to the Dalit. As the Dalit were denied access to education, Christian missionaries saw themselves as empowering the Dalit to rise up against their oppression.

Gutiérrez's "preferential option for the poor" is invoked by Prasad: "It is God who is with the poor and the oppressed." This is, naturally, based in Exodus: "the story of struggles for liberation from oppression, exploitation and injustice. It is the God of the Hebrews who has taken sides with the exploited masses. In a similar way He will take sides with Dalits too" (91). Prasad's use of the future tense—"He will take sides with Dalits too"—serves as a reminder that the Dalit have little to no history of resistance from which to draw encouragement or example. This is liberation theology at its most aspirational.

Fascinatingly, Prasad, unlike Gutiérrez or Cone, has to reckon with the need to actively remind his audience that they have access to the power of the Bible and theology, that they have the right, and even obligation, to call on these resources in their struggle. He cannot build on the foundation of the centuries of Catholic teaching in Latin America or of African American readings of the Bible; he has to start almost from the very beginning of the process: "Christians of Dalit origin, Tribals and other oppressed people who seek justice often forget or ignore their ground of oppression. . . .

To some extent Dalits and the oppressed do not seem to realize that the poor, orphans, and Dalits are the people close to God; they belong closely to God's liberation activity, they are the subjects of history and God's agents of transformation" (84). Thus Prasad's liberation theology takes us not only to a very different place and culture but to an earlier stage of the process.

In a remarkable essay entitled "Journeying with Moses toward True Solidarity: Shifting Social and Narrative Locations of the Oppressed and Their Liberator in Exodus 2–3," Bob Ekblad describes his experience of reading the Exodus story with Latino immigrants in a county jail in Washington State.[13] In this context, the oppressive Pharaoh figure is identifiable with the broad social structures that put so many young men, especially young men of color, in prison: addiction, inadequate employment opportunities, court-ordered fines, and so on. "The Israelite slaves and their Latino immigrant equivalents remain passive objects of Pharaoh's, and now our, perpetual domination system."[14] The power of that system is such that the inmates, like many others, assume that God inhabits a sort of space—"the privileged, luxury utopia of heaven"—so distant from their own.[15] They are mostly illegal immigrants, and therefore live on the margins of American society, ever at the mercy of a justice system that is all too willing to eliminate them from that society altogether.

Ekblad counters this sense of disempowerment by introducing his study group to a liberationist reading of the Exodus story, concentrating on the figure and call of Moses. He begins, however, by reorienting their understanding of God's role: not as a defender of the powerful but as an advocate for the vulnerable. This is demonstrated through the divine blessing bestowed on the midwives who saved the male Israelite infants from death, women who succeeded in spite of a legal system designed to oppress.

Moses—raised in Pharaoh's court, God's divinely ordained messenger—is not always an obvious or easily accessible model for the powerless. So Ekblad draws the inmates' attention to the fact that Moses is called by God not when he is in Egypt but when he is an exile, a fugitive from Egyptian justice, a wanderer in a foreign land. And he is there precisely because he broke the law "in solidarity with the oppressed."[16] The fact that Moses considers himself unfit for the task of implementing God's will provides yet another point of connection, especially for a community that has grown accustomed to seeing themselves as powerless. "God recruits unexpected people, common people," Ekblad writes. One of the inmates responds, "God works through humble people, people who are rejected, people with vices."[17]

The liberationist reading of the call of Moses thus provides Ekblad's imprisoned group a sense of potential, of purpose—of self-determination, even in a context where such empowerment appears to be truly impossible. Here is an example of liberation theology working not primarily toward a defined communal cause, be it economic or racial justice, but toward the inner transformation of the individual, toward a recognition that the God who called a fugitive Moses in the desert may well have a task for the incarcerated immigrant in modern America.

Our final example of liberation theology comes from the Native American community. In his essay "Canaanites,

Cowboys, and Indians: Deliverance, Conquest, and Liberation Theology Today," Robert Allen Warrior reflects on the attempt to include Native Americans in the liberation movement: "There are theologies of liberation for African Americans, Hispanic Americans, women, Asian Americans, even Jews. Why not Native Americans?"[18] Given the long history of Native American oppression, going back even further than the slave trade in America, the opportunity would seem to be there for the taking.

Warrior focuses the reader's attention on the colonialist impulse that underlies such attempts. "Liberals and conservatives alike have too often surveyed the conditions of Native Americans and decided to come to the rescue, always using their methods, their ideas, and their programs."[19] Where liberation theology has been most effective, it has always been deployed in the service of a community that was already implicated in the broader Judeo-Christian cultural context that was long primed to understand itself as Israel. Without such a context, the Exodus story may acquire a very different resonance.

The historical situation in which Native Americans encountered Christianity shaped their place in the narrative, and it was not the place of the Israelites. With the Puritans coming from their religiously oppressive Egypt to the promised land of America, the peoples who were already living there could hardly also be Israel. "The obvious characters in the story for Native Americans to identify with are the Canaanites," Warrior writes. "And, it is the Canaanite side of the story that has been overlooked by those seeking to articulate theologies of liberation."[20] This critique is eminently true: we have already noted that the liberation theologies of

Gutiérrez and Cone avoid direct treatment of the continued existence of slavery among the early Israelites. Even more notably absent is any mention whatsoever of the Canaanite peoples whom the Israelites are divinely commanded to slaughter—man, woman, and child.

This is a problem that complicates not only the anticipated end of the story but the very covenant that God makes with Israel at Sinai. Those who take the side of the Israelites often point to the laws protecting the vulnerable—the poor, the widow, the orphan—within Israelite society, seeing in these commands a sign of God's preferential option for the oppressed. But, as Warrior points out, these laws can be followed only once God has safely settled the Israelites in their land—that is, after the Canaanites have been eliminated from the scene. The God who liberates Israel is the same God who calls for the destruction of the Canaanites.

Even the Exodus story, a narrative of redemption from evil, has its victims. What is salvation to one group is violation or oppression to another. Warrior is inclined to set aside liberation theology, and indeed Christian theology altogether, as inappropriate to the task of bringing justice to the Native American community. As it is Christians who have done harm to that community for more than five hundred years, who can blame him? But he does point the way toward potential mechanisms for positive change. Primarily, he calls for Christian theology to place the Canaanites at the center of the narrative. "They are the last remaining ignored voice in the text," he writes; that is, they are the community displaced and marginalized by the movement of the Israelites from the margins to the center.[21] But he also gives a warning: one should not assume that what the Native

American community wants or needs is to be brought into the center of a story, a culture, and a theology that is not their own. "Christians, whether Native American or not, if they are to be involved, must learn how to participate in the struggle without making their story the whole story."[22] Liberation theology's intended universalism cannot be forced on the unwilling. We may identify with Israel, but we cannot replicate the sins of the past; we must live beside the Canaanites rather than forcibly dispossess or assimilate them.

Conclusion

Liberation theology is a fine place to end our exploration of the uses of the Exodus story. It brings together many of the themes that we have discussed: the reading of Exodus as commentary on the contemporary situation; the ever-changing identifications of a modern Egypt and Israel, Pharaoh and Moses; and, above all, the use of Exodus to give definition and purpose to a community. Liberation theology reveals that the power of the Exodus story can be expressed in both faith and practice, in theological inquiry and in lived action. The themes that liberation theology highlights are those that have always been central to Exodus: oppression and redemption, the work of the divine in human history, and the omnipresent hope for a better future.

In liberation theology we also see, as we have so many times elsewhere, the inherent and extraordinary flexibility of the Exodus story. It can be appropriated by virtually all peoples in all times and places who are suffering from oppression, defined in any number of ways. And liberation theology makes explicit something that is true everywhere, though not always recognized: every reading of the Exodus story is a reading into the Exodus story. The Exodus story both defines us and is defined by us, provides meaning for its readers and is given meaning by the act of reading it. It is flexible because we make it so—but we choose it, over other stories, because it contains the crystallization of humanity's deepest desires: for justice, for freedom, for self-determination.

The various appropriations of Exodus are not always neat and tidy; there is no such thing as a perfect parallel. It is thus incumbent on us to use the biblical narrative with care, to read it and ourselves with a critical eye—not to undermine the story's power but to recognize how we are using it for our own purposes, and to use it responsibly.

The story's power cannot be denied. It has been a central part of our tradition for three thousand years, and we would not be who we are—whoever we are—without it. We cannot put it any better than Croatto does, so joyfully: "Is not the Exodus theme of immense hermeneutical richness?"[23]

CHAPTER 1: BEFORE THE BIBLE

1. For a recent argument on this topic, see Richard Elliott Friedman, *The Exodus: How It Happened and Why It Matters* (New York: HarperOne, 2017).

2. For the fullest treatment of this idea, see Konrad Schmid, *Genesis and the Moses Story: Israel's Dual Origins* (Winona Lake, IN: Eisenbrauns, 2010).

3. Papyrus Anastasi V, in William W. Hallo, ed., *The Context of Scripture* (Leiden: Brill, 2002), 3:16.

4. On the form and identity of early Israel, see especially Israel Finkelstein, *The Archaeology of the Israelite Settlement* (Jerusalem: Israel Exploration Society, 1988).

5. Biblical quotations throughout the book are based on the *Tanakh: The New Jewish Publication Society according to the Traditional Hebrew Text* (NJPS) and the New Revised Standard Version (NRSV). I have made a few editorial changes to quotes from the NJPS, most commonly by lowercasing divine pronouns and possessive pronouns and substituting "Yahweh" for "the LORD."

6. See the seminal work of Gerhard von Rad, "The Form-Critical Problem of the Hexateuch," in *The Problem of the Hexateuch and Other Essays* (New York: McGraw-Hill, 1966), 1–78.

7. For the Laws of Eshnunna, see Martha Roth, *Law Collections from Mesopotamia and Asia Minor* (Atlanta: Scholars, 1997).

8. See Dennis Pardee, *Ritual and Cult at Ugarit* (Atlanta: Society of Biblical Literature, 2002).

9. See the work of Menahem Haran, including "The Size of Books in the Bible and the Division of the Pentateuch and

the Prophets: Paleographical and Compositional Aspects in the Arrangement of the Biblical Collection," *Tarbiz* 53 (1984): 329–52 (in Hebrew).

10. For the following, see Joel S. Baden, *The Composition of the Pentateuch: Renewing the Documentary Hypothesis* (New Haven: Yale University Press, 2012).

11. See Jeffrey Stackert, "Pentateuch Coherence and the Science of Reading," in *The Formation of the Pentateuch,* ed. Jan C. Gertz et al. (Tübingen: Mohr Siebeck, 2016), 253–68.

CHAPTER 2: THE EXODUS STORY OUTSIDE THE BOOK OF EXODUS

1. On the Wisdom of Solomon, see Samuel Cheon, *The Exodus Story in the Wisdom of Solomon: A Study in Biblical Interpretation* (Sheffield, UK: Sheffield Academic Press, 1997).

2. On the Exodus story in Josephus, see Giovanni Frulla, "Reconstructing Exodus Tradition: Moses in the Second Book of Josephus' *Antiquities*," in *Flavius Josephus: Interpretation and History*, ed. Jack Pastor, Pnina Stern, and Menahem Mor (Leiden: Brill, 2011), 111–24; Paul Spilsbury, "Exodus in Josephus," in *The Book of Exodus: Composition, Reception, and Interpretation*, ed. Thomas B. Dozeman, Craig A. Evans, and Joel N. Lohr (Leiden: Brill, 2014), 465–84.

3. On Philo's use of Exodus, see Louis Feldman, *Philo's Portrayal of Moses in the Context of Ancient Judaism* (Notre Dame: University of Notre Dame Press, 2007); Gregory Sterling, "The People of the Covenant or the People of God: Exodus in Philo of Alexandria," in *The Book of Exodus*, ed. Dozeman, Evans, and Lohr, 404–39.

4. Dale C. Allison, Jr., *The New Moses: A Matthean Typology* (Minneapolis: Fortress, 1993), 272.

5. See Craig A. Evans, "Exodus in the New Testament: Patterns of Revelation and Redemption," in *The Book of Exodus*, ed. Dozeman, Evans, and Lohr, 448–51.

6. For the following, see Allison, *The New Moses*.

7. Ibid., 268.

8. Ibid., 278.

9. On Exodus in the Gospel of John, see Wayne A. Meeks, *The Prophet-King: Moses Traditions and the Johannine Christology* (Leiden: Brill, 1967).

10. Ibid., 294.

11. On Paul's use of Exodus in Corinthians, see Carla Swafford Works, *The Church in the Wilderness: Paul's Use of Exodus Traditions in 1 Corinthians* (Tübingen: Mohr Siebeck, 2014).

CHAPTER 3: EXODUS AS RITUAL

1. See Bezalel Porten, "The Passover Letter," in Hallo, *The Context of Scripture*, 3:116–17.

2. See J. B. Segal, *The Hebrew Passover: From the Earliest Times to A.D. 70* (London: Oxford University Press, 1963).

3. For the following, see Baruch M. Bokser, *The Origins of the Seder: The Passover Rite and Early Rabbinic Judaism* (Berkeley: University of California Press, 1984); Lawrence A. Hoffman and David Arnow, eds., *My People's Passover Haggadah: Traditional Texts, Modern Commentaries* (Woodstock, VT: Jewish Lights, 2008).

4. Quoted in Bokser, *The Origins of the Seder*, 81.

5. Quoted in Hoffman and Arnow, *My People's Passover Haggadah*, 1:23.

6. See, for example, Joachim Jeremias, *The Eucharistic Words of Jesus* (Philadelphia: Fortress, 1966), 60.

7. Irenaeus, *The Demonstration of the Apostolic Preaching*, 25; quoted in Raniero Cantalamessa, *Easter in the Early Church: An Anthology of Jewish and Early Christian Texts* (Collegeville, MN: Liturgical Press, 1993), 50–51.

8. Origen, *Commentary on John*, 110; quoted in Cantalamessa, *Easter in the Early Church*, 54.

9. Origen, *Homilies on Numbers* 23, 6; quoted in Cantalamessa, *Easter in the Early Church*, 56–57.

10. For the following, see especially Paul F. Bradshaw, "The Origins of Easter," in Paul F. Bradshaw and Lawrence A.

Hoffman, eds., *Passover and Easter: Origin and History to Modern Times* (Notre Dame: University of Notre Dame Press, 1999), 81–97.

11. Eusebius, *On the Paschal Solemnity*, 7; quoted in Cantalamessa, *Easter in the Early Church*, 68.

12. Martin Luther, "On the Babylonish Captivity of the Church," Christian Classics Ethereal Library, https://www.ccel.org/.

CHAPTER 4: SINAI AND THE LAW

1. Ephraim E. Urbach, *The Sages: Their Concepts and Beliefs* (Jerusalem: Magnes, 1987), 317.

2. See Christine Hayes, *What's Divine about Divine Law? Early Perspectives* (Princeton: Princeton University Press, 2015), 246–86.

3. Urbach, *The Sages*, 386–87.

4. Hayes, *What's Divine*, 256; italics in the original.

5. Ibid., 259.

6. See, for example, *b. B.M.* 59b.

7. On Paul and the law, see James D. G. Dunn, *The New Perspective on Paul*, 2nd ed. (Grand Rapids, MI: Eerdmans, 2008); E. P. Sanders, *Paul, the Law, and the Jewish People* (Philadelphia: Fortress, 1983); Luke Timothy Johnson, "Law in Early Christianity," in *Christianity and the Law: An Introduction*, ed. John Witte, Jr., and Frank S. Alexander (Cambridge: Cambridge University Press, 2008), 53–70.

8. Dunn, *The New Perspective*, 150.

9. Robert Grant, "The Decalogue in Early Christianity," *HTR* 60 (1947): 16.

10. On the various identifications of the Minim, see Ruth Langer, *Cursing the Christians? A History of the Birkat HaMinim* (New York: Oxford University Press, 2012).

11. Ephraim E. Urbach, "The Decalogue in Jewish Worship," in *The Ten Commandments in History and Tradition*, ed. Ben-Zion Segal (Jerusalem: Magnes, 1990), 179–81.

12. Cited in ibid., 187.

13. Martin Luther, *Table Talk*, 271, Christian Classics Ethereal Library (CCEL), https://www.ccel.org/.
14. Leivy Smolar and Moses Aberbach, "The Golden Calf Episode in Postbiblical Literature," *HUCA* 39 (1968): 99.
15. Ibid., 100.
16. Moshe Halbertal and Avishai Margalit, *Idolatry* (Cambridge: Harvard University Press, 1992), 241.
17. Urbach, "The Decalogue," 175.

CHAPTER 5: SOCIAL FORMATION
AND COMMUNAL IDENTITY

1. Luther, *Table Talk*, 244.
2. Ibid., 49.
3. Martin Luther, *On the Enslaved Will*, 51, Christian Classics Ethereal Library, https://www.ccel.org/.
4. Ibid., 45.
5. John Calvin, *Institutes* 4.8.1, Christian Classics Ethereal Library, https://www.ccel.org/.
6. Ibid., 4.11.8.
7. John Calvin, *Harmony of the Four Last Books of Moses*, on Exodus 5:2, in *Commentaries on the Four Last Books of Moses arranged in the Form of a Harmony* (Grand Rapids, MI: Baker, 1979).
8. Ibid., on Exodus 8:25.
9. Ibid.
10. Ibid., on Exodus 1:15.
11. Ibid., on Exodus 3:2.
12. John Knox, *On Rebellion*, ed. Roger A. Mason (Cambridge: Cambridge University Press, 1994), 52.
13. Quoted in Simon Schama, *The Embarrassment of Riches: An Interpretation of Dutch Culture in the Golden Age* (Berkeley: University of California Press, 1988), 105.
14. Ibid., 113.
15. Anthony D. Smith, *The Nation Made Real: Art and National Identity in Western Europe, 1600–1850* (Oxford: Oxford University Press, 2013), 38–39.

16. Schama, *Embarrassment of Riches*, 113.

17. Quoted in Geert H. Janssen, *The Dutch Revolt and Catholic Exile in Reformation Europe* (Cambridge: Cambridge University Press, 2014), 55.

18. Ibid., 54.

19. William Turner, *The Hunting and Fyndyng out of the Romish Fox* (London: John W. Parker, 1851), 19.

20. Janel Mueller, ed., *Katherine Parr: Complete Works and Correspondence* (Chicago: University of Chicago Press, 2011), 468.

21. Justine Walden, "The Maps in the English Geneva Bible," in *Shaping the Bible in the Reformation*, ed. Bruce Gordon and Matthew McLean (Leiden: Brill, 2012), 198.

22. Quotes from Cartwright are taken from John Ayre, ed., *The Works of John Whitgift* (Cambridge: Cambridge University Press, 1851), 26.

23. Quoted in John Coffey, *Exodus and Liberation: Deliverance Politics from John Calvin to Martin Luther King, Jr.* (Oxford: Oxford University Press, 2013), 39.

24. Ibid., 39.

25. Ibid., 47.

26. Ibid., 48.

27. Ibid., 39–53.

28. Dom Wolfe et al., ed., *The Complete Prose Works of John Milton*, 8 vols. (New Haven: Yale University Press, 1953–82), 4.1.386–87.

29. Harold Paget, *Bradford's History of the Plymouth Settlement, 1608–1650* (New York: E. P. Dutton, 1920), 17.

30. Quoted in Avihu Zakai, *Exile and Kingdom: History and Apocalypse in the Puritan Migration to America* (Cambridge: Cambridge University Press, 1992), 65.

31. Jonathan Boyarin, "Reading Exodus into History," *New Literary History* 23 (1992): 537.

32. John Cotton, *God's Promise to His Plantations* (London: William Jones, 1634).

33. William Brigham, ed., *The Compact with the Charter and Laws of the Colony of New Plymouth* (Boston: Dutton and Wentworth, 1836), 3.

34. *Collections of the Massachusetts Historical Society for the Year 1792* (Boston: Munroe & Francis, 1806), 1:246.

35. See Alfred A. Cave, "Canaanites in a Promised Land: The American Indian and the Providential Theory of Empire," *American Indian Quarterly* 12 (1988): 277–97.

36. Thomas Jefferson, "A Summary View of British Rights in America," 1774, Thomas Jefferson Library Collection, Library of Congress, https://www.loc.gov/item/08016823/.

37. Elijah Fitch, *A Discourse, the Substance of which was delivered at Hopkinton, on the Lord's-Day, March 24th, 1776, being the next Sabbath following the Precipitate Flight of the British troops from Boston* (Boston: John Boyle, 1776).

38. Nicholas Street, "The American States Acting Over the Part of the Children of Israel into the Wilderness and Thereby Impeding Their Entrance into Canaan's Rest" (1777), in Conrad Cherry, *God's New Israel: Religious Interpretations of American Destiny* (Chapel Hill: University of North Carolina Press, 2014), 70.

39. James P. Byrd, *Sacred Scripture, Sacred War: The Bible and the American Revolution* (Oxford: Oxford University Press, 2013), 51.

40. Ezra Stiles, "The United States Elevated to Glory and Honour" (1783), in Cherry, *God's New Israel*, 83.

41. Samuel Langdon, "The Republic of the Israelites as an Example to the American States" (1788), in Cherry, *God's New Israel*, 96–97.

42. See Robert P. Hay, "George Washington: American Moses," *American Quarterly* 21 (1969): 780–91.

43. Byrd, *Sacred Scripture*, 65.

44. Cyprian Strong, *A discourse, delivered at Hebron, at the celebration of the anniversary of American independence, July 4th, 1799* (Hartford: Hudson and Goodwin, 1799).

45. Quoted in Byrd, *Sacred Scripture*, 70.

46. Ebenezer Gay, *An oration, pronounced at Suffield, on Saturday the 22'd of Feb. A.D. 1800: The day recommended by Congress, for the people to assemble, publicly to testify their grief, for the death of General George Washington* (Suffield: Edward Gray, 1800).

47. Quoted in Leonard J. Arrington, *Brigham Young: American Moses* (New York: Knopf, 1985).

48. Quoted in S. Scott Rohrer, *Wandering Souls: Protestant Migrations in America, 1630–1865* (Chapel Hill: University of North Carolina Press, 2010), 243.

49. Quoted in ibid., 232.

50. Quoted in Matthew Burton Bowman, *The Mormon People: The Making of an American Faith* (New York: Random House, 2012), 94.

51. Arrington, *Brigham Young*, 127.

52. Ibid., 156.

53. Ibid., 174.

54. Quoted in John G. Turner, *Brigham Young: Pioneer Prophet* (Cambridge: Harvard University Press, 2012), 148.

55. Edward Tullidge, *Life of Brigham Young; or, Utah and Her Founders* (New York: [s.n.], 1876).

CHAPTER 6: EXODUS AND CIVIL RIGHTS

1. Samuel Sewall, *The Selling of Joseph: A Memorial* (Boston: Bartholomew Green and John Allen, 1700).

2. Granville Sharp, *The Law of Retribution; or, A Serious Warning to Great Britain and Her Colonies, Founded on Unquestionable Examples of God's Temporal Vengeance against Tyrants, Slave-Holders, and Oppressors* (London: W. Richardson, 1776).

3. Nathaniel Niles, *Two Discourses on Liberty; delivered at the North Church, in Newbury-port, on Lord's-Day, June 5th, 1774, and published at the general desire of the hearers* (Newbury-Port, MA: I. Thomas and H. W. Tinges, 1774).

4. Levi Hart, *Liberty described and recommended; in a sermon, preached to the Corporation of Freemen in Farmington, at their meeting on Tuesday, September 20, 1774, and published at their desire* (Hartford, CT: Eben. Watson, 1775).

5. Julian D. Mason, Jr., ed., *The Poems of Phillis Wheatley* (Chapel Hill: University of North Carolina Press, 1989), 203–4.

6. Richard Allen, *The Life, Experience, and Gospel Labours of the Rt. Rev. Richard Allen* (Philadelphia: Martin & Boden, 1833), 45, 49.

7. Caesar Sarter, "Essay on Slavery," *Essex Journal and Merrimack Packet*, August 17, 1774.

8. Coffey, *Exodus and Liberation*, 97.

9. Albert J. Raboteau, "African Americans, Exodus, and the American Israel," in *Religion and American Culture: A Reader*, ed. David G. Hackett (New York: Routledge, 2003), 76.

10. Ibid., 79.

11. Absalom Jones, *A Thanksgiving Sermon, preached January 1, 1808, in St. Thomas's, or the African Episcopal, Church, Philadelphia* (Philadelphia: Fry and Kammerer, 1808); the quotes in this paragraph are taken from this source.

12. Quoted in Raboteau, "African Americans," 83.

13. David Walker, *Walker's Appeal, in Four Articles* (Boston: David Walker, 1830).

14. Eddie Glaude, Jr., *Exodus! Religion, Race, and Nation in Early Nineteenth-Century Black America* (Chicago: University of Chicago Press, 2000), 56.

15. Quoted in Nicholas Guyatt, *Providence and the Invention of the United States, 1607–1876* (Cambridge: Cambridge University Press, 2007), 188.

16. Quoted in Rhondda Robinson Thomas, *Claiming Exodus: A Cultural History of Afro-Atlantic Identity* (Waco, TX: Baylor University Press, 2012), 44.

17. Glaude, *Exodus!*, 124–25.

18. Henry Highland Garnet, "An Address to the Slaves of the United States of America, Buffalo, N.Y., 1843," *Electronic*

Texts in American Studies, 8, http://digitalcommons.unl.edu /etas/8.

19. John Rock, "What If the Slaves Are Emancipated?," *Liberator*, February 4, 1862.

20. Quoted in Coffey, *Exodus and Liberation*, 135.

21. Henry Ward Beecher, *Freedom and War: Discourses on Topics Suggested by the Times* (Boston: Ticknor and Fields, 1863), 90.

22. Quoted in Coffey, *Exodus and Liberation*, 140.

23. Ibid., 184.

24. Eulogy on Henry Clay, July 6, 1952, in Roy Basler, ed., *The Collected Works of Abraham Lincoln*, vol. 2 (New Brunswick: Rutgers University Press, 1953), 132.

25. Matthew Simpson, *Funeral Address Delivered at the Burial of President Lincoln at Springfield, Illinois, May 4, 1865* (New York: Carlton & Porter, 1865).

26. *Liberator*, November 1, 1861.

27. Henry Turner, "The Plagues of This Country," *Christian Recorder*, July 12, 1862.

28. *Daily Dispatch*, November 6, 1863.

29. Benjamin Palmer, "National Responsibility before God," in Cherry, *God's New Israel*, 184.

30. Clergy of the Confederate States of America, *Address to Christians Throughout the World* (London: Strangeways and Walden, 1863), 5.

31. Henry Highland Garnet, "Let the Monster Perish," BlackPost.org, February 12, 1865, https://blackpast.org/1865 -henry-highland-garnet-let-monster-perish.

32. Ibid.

33. Ibid.

34. Mark Noll, "The Bible and Slavery," in *Religion and the American Civil War*, ed. Randall M. Miller, Harry S. Stout, and Charles Reagan Wilson (Oxford: Oxford University Press, 1998), 44.

35. Ibid., 45.

36. Ibid., 52.

37. Quoted in Herbert Robinson Marbury, *Pillars of Cloud and Fire: The Politics of Exodus in African American Biblical Interpretation* (New York: New York University Press, 2015), 152.

38. Ibid., 153.

39. Gary S. Selby, *Martin Luther King and the Rhetoric of Freedom: The Exodus Narrative in America's Struggle for Civil Rights* (Waco: Baylor University Press, 2008), 55.

40. Ibid., 83.

41. Ibid., 72.

42. Ibid., 77.

43. Ibid., 84.

44. Malcolm X, speech at the Harlem Freedom Rally, 1960, Malcolm X collection, http://malcolmxfiles.blogspot.com /2013/05/harlem-freedom-rally-1960.html.

45. Quoted in Coffey, *Exodus and Liberation*, 182.

46. Marbury, *Pillars*, 160.

47. Barack Obama, speech in Jerusalem, March 21, 2013. Transcript published in the *New York Times*, March 22, 2013.

CHAPTER 7: LIBERATION THEOLOGY

1. Gustavo Gutiérrez, *A Theology of Liberation: History, Politics, and Salvation*, rev. ed. (London: SCM, 1988); further references to this source are given by page number in the text.

2. J. Severino Croatto, *Exodus: A Hermeneutics of Freedom* (Maryknoll, VT: Orbis, 1981); further references to this source are given by page number in the text.

3. George Pixley, *On Exodus: A Liberation Perspective* (Maryknoll, VT: Orbis, 1988), 81.

4. Jon D. Levenson, *The Hebrew Bible, the Old Testament, and Historical Criticism* (Louisville, KY: Westminster John Knox, 1993), 134.

5. Ibid., 157.

6. James H. Cone, *A Black Theology of Liberation: Fortieth Anniversary Edition* (Maryknoll, VT: Orbis, 2010); further references to this source are given by page number in the text.

7. James H. Cone, *God of the Oppressed*, rev. ed. (Maryknoll, VT: Orbis, 1997), 91.

8. Ibid.

9. Ibid.

10. Ibid., xi.

11. Ibid., xii.

12. D. Manohar Chandra Prasad, *The Book of Exodus and Dalit Liberation* (Bangalore: Asian Trading Corporation, 2005); further references to this source are given by page number in the text.

13. Bob Ekblad, "Journeying with Moses toward True Solidarity: Shifting Social and Narrative Locations of the Oppressed and Their Liberator in Exodus 2–3," in *Reading Other-wise: Socially Engaged Biblical Scholars Reading with Their Local Communities,* ed. Gerald O. West (Leiden: Brill, 2007), 87–102.

14. Ibid., 88.

15. Ibid., 89.

16. Ibid., 96.

17. Ibid., 100.

18. Robert Allen Warrior, "Canaanites, Cowboys, and Indians: Deliverance, Conquest, and Liberation Theology Today," in *Native and Christian: Indigenous Voices on Religious Identity in the United States and Canada*, ed. James Treat (New York: Routledge, 1996), 94.

19. Ibid.

20. Ibid., 95.

21. Ibid., 98.

22. Ibid., 99.

23. Croatto, *Exodus*, 30.

Allison, Dale C., Jr. *The New Moses: A Matthean Typology.*
    Minneapolis: Fortress, 1993.

Arrington, Leonard J. *Brigham Young: American Moses.* New
    York: Knopf, 1985.

Barlow, Philip. *Mormons and the Bible: The Place of the Latter-day
    Saints in American Religion.* Oxford: Oxford University
    Press, 2013.

Bokser, Baruch M. *The Origins of the Seder: The Passover Rite and
    Early Rabbinic Judaism.* Berkeley: University of California
    Press, 1984.

Boyarin, Jonathan. "Reading Exodus into History." *New Literary
    History* 23 (1992): 523–54.

Bradshaw, Paul F., and Lawrence A. Hoffman, eds. *Passover and
    Easter: Origin and History to Modern Times.* Notre Dame:
    University of Notre Dame Press, 1999.

Brague, Rémi. *The Law of God: The Philosophical History of an
    Idea.* Chicago: University of Chicago Press, 2007.

Byrd, James P. *Sacred Scripture, Sacred War: The Bible and the
    American Revolution.* Oxford: Oxford University Press, 2013.

Cantalamessa, Raniero. *Easter in the Early Church: An Anthol-
    ogy of Jewish and Early Christian Texts.* Collegeville, MN:
    Liturgical Press, 1993.

Cave, Alfred A. "Canaanites in a Promised Land: The American
    Indian and the Providential Theory of Empire." *American
    Indian Quarterly* 12 (1988): 277–97.

Cheon, Samuel. *The Exodus Story in the Wisdom of Solomon: A
    Study in Biblical Interpretation.* Sheffield, UK: Sheffield
    Academic Press, 1997.

Cherry, Conrad. *God's New Israel: Religious Interpretations of America's Destiny*. Chapel Hill: University of North Carolina Press, 2014.

Coffey, John. *Exodus and Liberation: Deliverance Politics from John Calvin to Martin Luther King, Jr.* Oxford: Oxford University Press, 2013.

Cone, James H. *A Black Theology of Liberation: Fortieth Anniversary Edition*. Maryknoll, NY: Orbis, 2010.

————. *God of the Oppressed*. Rev. ed. Maryknoll, NY: Orbis, 1997.

Croatto, J. Severino. *Exodus: A Hermeneutics of Freedom*. Maryknoll, NY: Orbis, 1981.

Dozeman, Thomas B., Craig A. Evans, and Joel N. Lohr, eds. *The Book of Exodus: Composition, Reception, and Interpretation*. Leiden: Brill, 2014.

Dunn, James D. G. *The New Perspective on Paul*. 2nd ed. Grand Rapids, MI: Eerdmans, 2008.

Ekblad, Bob. "Journeying with Moses toward True Solidarity: Shifting Social and Narrative Locations of the Oppressed and Their Liberator in Exodus 2–3." In *Reading Other-wise: Socially Engaged Biblical Scholars Reading with Their Local Communities*, edited by Gerald O. West, 87–102. Leiden: Brill, 2007.

Evans, Craig A. "Exodus in the New Testament: Patterns of Revelation and Redemption." In *The Book of Exodus*, edited by Dozeman, Evans, and Lohr, 440–64.

Feldman, Louis. *Philo's Portrayal of Moses in the Context of Ancient Judaism*. Notre Dame: University of Notre Dame Press, 2007.

Friedman, Richard Elliott. *The Exodus: How It Happened and Why It Matters*. New York: HarperOne, 2017.

Frulla, Giovanni. "Reconstructing Exodus Tradition: Moses in the Second Book of Josephus' *Antiquities*." In *Flavius Josephus: Interpretation and History*, edited by Jack Pastor, Pnina Stern, and Menahem Mor, 111–24. Leiden: Brill, 2011.

Glaude, Eddie S., Jr. *Exodus! Religion, Race, and Nation in Early Nineteenth-Century Black America*. Chicago: University of Chicago Press, 2000.

Grant, Robert. "The Decalogue in Early Christianity." *Harvard Theological Review* 60 (1947): 1–17.

Gutiérrez, Gustavo. *A Theology of Liberation: History, Politics, and Salvation.* Rev. ed. London: SCM, 1988.

Halbertal, Moshe, and Avishai Margalit. *Idolatry.* Cambridge: Harvard University Press, 1992.

Hallo, William W., ed. *The Context of Scripture.* Vol. 3. Leiden: Brill, 2002.

Hay, Robert P. "George Washington: American Moses." *American Quarterly* 21 (1969): 780–91.

Hayes, Christine. *What's Divine about Divine Law? Early Perspectives.* Princeton: Princeton University Press, 2015.

Hoffman, Lawrence A., and David Arnow, eds. *My People's Passover Haggadah: Traditional Texts, Modern Commentaries.* Woodstock, VT: Jewish Lights, 2008.

Janssen, Geert H. *The Dutch Revolt and Catholic Exile in Reformation Europe.* Cambridge: Cambridge University Press, 2014.

Jeremias, Joachim. *The Eucharistic Words of Jesus.* Philadelphia: Fortress, 1966.

Johnson, Luke Timothy. "Law in Early Christianity." In *Christianity and the Law: An Introduction,* edited by John Witte, Jr., and Frank S. Alexander, 53–70. Cambridge: Cambridge University Press, 2008.

Levenson, Jon D. *The Hebrew Bible, the Old Testament, and Historical Criticism.* Louisville, KY: Westminster John Knox, 1993.

Marbury, Herbert Robinson. *Pillars of Cloud and Fire: The Politics of Exodus in African American Biblical Interpretation.* New York: New York University Press, 2015.

Meeks, Wayne A. *The Prophet-King: Moses Traditions and the Johannine Christology.* Leiden: Brill, 1967.

Noll, Mark A. "The Bible and Slavery." In *Religion and the American Civil War,* edited by Randall M. Miller, Harry S. Stout, and Charles Reagan Wilson, 43–73. Oxford: Oxford University Press, 1998.

Prasad, D. Manohar Chandra. *The Book of Exodus and Dalit Liberation.* Bangalore: Asian Trading Corporation, 2005.

Raboteau, Albert J. "African Americans, Exodus, and the American Israel." In *Religion and American Culture: A Reader*, edited by David G. Hackett, 75–87. New York: Routledge, 2003.

Rohrer, S. Scott. *Wandering Souls: Protestant Migrations in America, 1630–1865*. Chapel Hill: University of North Carolina Press, 2010.

Sanders, E. P. *Paul, the Law, and the Jewish People*. Philadelphia: Fortress, 1983.

Schama, Simon. *The Embarrassment of Riches: An Interpretation of Dutch Culture in the Golden Age*. Berkeley: University of California Press, 1988.

Segal, Ben-Zion, ed. *The Ten Commandments in History and Tradition*. Jerusalem: Magnes, 1985.

Segal, J. B. *The Hebrew Passover: From the Earliest Times to A.D. 70*. London: Oxford University Press, 1963.

Selby, Gary S. *Martin Luther King and the Rhetoric of Freedom: The Exodus Narrative in America's Struggle for Civil Rights*. Waco, TX: Baylor University Press, 2008.

Smith, Anthony D. *The Nation Made Real: Art and National Identity in Western Europe, 1600–1850*. Oxford: Oxford University Press, 2013.

Smolar, Leivy, and Moses Aberbach. "The Golden Calf Episode in Postbiblical Literature." *Hebrew Union College Annual* 39 (1968): 91–116.

Spilsbury, Paul. "Exodus in Josephus." In *The Book of Exodus*, edited by Dozeman, Evans, and Lohr, 465–84.

Sterling, Gregory. "The People of the Covenant or the People of God: Exodus in Philo of Alexandria." In *The Book of Exodus*, edited by Dozeman, Evans, and Lohr, 404–39.

Thomas, Rhondda Robinson. *Claiming Exodus: A Cultural History of Afro-Atlantic Identity*. Waco, TX: Baylor University Press, 2012.

Tullidge, Edward. *Life of Brigham Young; or, Utah and Her Founders*. New York: [s.n.], 1876.

Urbach, Ephraim E. "The Decalogue in Jewish Worship." In *The Ten Commandments in History and Tradition*, ed. Ben-Zion Segal, 179–81.

———. *The Sages: Their Concepts and Beliefs*. Jerusalem: Magnes, 1987.

Walden, Justine. "The Maps in the English Geneva Bible." In *Shaping the Bible in the Reformation*, edited by Bruce Gordon and Matthew McLean, 187–216. Leiden: Brill, 2012.

Walzer, Michael. *Exodus and Revolution*. New York: Basic, 1985.

Warrior, Robert Allen. "Canaanites, Cowboys, and Indians: Deliverance, Conquest, and Liberation Theology Today." In *Native and Christian: Indigenous Voices on Religious Identity in the United States and Canada*, edited by James Treat, 93–100. New York: Routledge, 1996.

Works, Carla Swafford. *The Church in the Wilderness: Paul's Use of Exodus Traditions in 1 Corinthians*. Tübingen: Mohr Siebeck, 2014.

Zakai, Avihu. *Exile and Kingdom: History and Apocalypse in the Puritan Migration to America*. Cambridge: Cambridge University Press, 1992.